SCOTCH OBSESSIONS

SCOTCH OBSESSIONS

Brian D. Osborne
and Ronald Armstrong

Birlinn

Acknowledgement
The extracts from Anthony Powell's poem *Caledonia* appears
by permission of the author.

First published in Great Britain, 1996 by
Birlinn Limited
14 High Street
Edinburgh EH1 1TE

ISBN 1-874744-68-8

British Library Cataloguing-in-Publication Data
A Catalogue record of this book is available
from the British Library

Designed and typeset in 11/13pt Berkeley
by Janet Watson

Made and printed in Finland by
Werner Söderström OY

Contents

Introduction

What is a "Scotch Obsession"?

The detailed answer will, we hope, be found in the pages of this book – but in general what we have defined as "Obsessions" are beliefs, habits of mind and tendencies that the Scots, or the world in general, take to be more than just simply typical of the nation but which are major elements in the creation of the national image and the formation of the national character. Some of these "Obsessions" are perceived more clearly by foreign onlookers – the suggestion that the Scottish people are obsessed by money is, for one reason or another, more often made by outsiders than by Scots. Others, such as an obsession with the United States of America (a preoccupation extending from the eighteenth century to the present day and embracing such disparate phenomena as emigration, moving pictures and Country & Western music) are much more clearly seen by Scots than by outsiders. Of course there is a broad common ground where perceptions are shared – both Scots and foreigners would probably identify England, drink and religion as ripe ground for the identification and exploration of obsession; some might indeed consider that these three obsessions sum up all that there is to say about Scotland. It could be taken as an encouraging sign of the richness and diversity of Scotland that we had no difficulty in identifying at least eighteen major "Scotch Obsessions" – or it may give cause for deep concern about the mental health of the nation.

One of the fascinations of studying these "Scotch Obsessions" has been discovering how enduring they have proved to be. Tendencies that one can detect as major influences in contemporary Scotland time and again prove to have very deep roots – which is just perhaps another way of acknowledging that an obsession cannot be simply some passing fad or fancy but must reflect a persistent and deep-seated preoccupation of lasting significance to the nation.

As a consequence of the long-standing nature and mass appeal of these obsessions they have inevitably provided wonderful raw material for many of our poets, novelists, dramatists, philosophers and scholars and our reflections on the "Scotch Obsessions" have been reinforced by extracts and examples from Scotch savants ranging from John Barbour (1320–1395) to Bill Shankly (1913–1981)

Our title, it must be admitted, is itself something of an obsession. Well-meaning experts will say that "Scotch" should only be applied as an adjective before eggs, marmalade, shortbread and whisky and that in all other cases the forms Scots or Scottish are to be preferred. This is simply nonsense. The use of Scotch as a generally applied term has good authority and is of long pedigree. Dr. Johnson, to cite a leading English prose stylist, wrote:

> But, Sir, let me tell you, the noblest prospect which a
> Scotchman ever sees, is the high road that leads him
> to England!

North of the Border, Walter Scott happily and interchangeably used all three forms, and Robert Burns was more than content to publish *Poems, chiefly in the Scottish Dialect*, contribute to the *Scots Musical Museum* and write *On a Scotch Bard Gone to the West Indies*. Official warrant for the "Scotch" form can be found in, for example, the formation of the "Scotch Education Department" in 1872. It is only in the twentieth century that false gentility and ill-substantiated pedantry has made "Scotch" generally unacceptable. It would have been perfectly possible to have called this book "Scots Obsessions" or, perhaps less mellifluously, "Scottish Obsessions" – we however chose to call it "Scotch Obsessions" for two reasons. One is that, to us, this form sounds best, the other was the sheer delight of contradiction and the pleasure of annoying many readers. Is thrawnness, perversity and a delight in controversy not itself a very "Scotch Obsession"?

Brian D. Osborne and Ronald Armstrong
May 1996

OLD MORTALITY

The Scots and Death

Death can hardly be claimed to be uniquely Scottish – Benjamin Franklin reminded us that "in this world nothing can be said to be certain, except death and taxes" – and death is the end of us all. However the Scots can certainly be felt to have a particular relationship with the "last enemy". One of the most familiar of Scottish toasts reminds the listener both of the inevitability of death and suggests something of a characteristically robust Scottish attitude to death:

Here's tae us!
Wha's like us?
Damn few!
And they're a' deid!

This unsentimental attitude is reflected in a story told by Dean Ramsay in his *Reminiscences of Scottish Life & Character*. An old shoemaker is sitting by the bedside of his dying wife.

"John," says she, "ye maun promise me to bury me in the auld kirk-yard at Stra'von, beside my mither. I couldna rest in peace among unco folk, in the dirt and smoke o' Glasgow." "Weel, weel, Jenny, my woman," said John, soothingly, "we'll just pit you in the Gorbals first, and gin ye dinna lie quiet, we'll try ye sine in Stra'von."

Jenny doubtless, like many Scotswomen of an earlier age had, carefully, tucked away a best pair of sheets for the "laying out" and would have had a concern, amounting almost to an obsession, about the need for a decent and respectable funeral.

The Scottish funeral has been celebrated widely and justly. Admittedly some of the incidents recorded seem at times lacking in respect for the dead, perhaps because it was the custom in many areas for bodies to be carried considerable distances and the funeral party expected, required and received ample refreshment. This doubtless explains the Speyside funeral where when the funeral party arrived, belatedly, at the kirk-yard everything was ready and waiting – save for the coffin. This, it was discovered, had been placed on a dyke outside an inn along the way while the mourners had gone inside for a restorative whisky. When they emerged, refreshed and strengthened, they marched on happily – but unfortunately forgot to bring the coffin along.

These more extreme examples would seem to have died out with the advent of the more "respectable" Victorian age, and by the turn of the century the funeral had become a highly formalised ritual. The development of exclusive burial grounds, like Glasgow's Necropolis – literally the city of the dead – and their elaborate funerary monuments was a notable feature of the period. On a humbler level, one of the chief attractions of the many friendly societies which sprang up in the nineteenth century and attracted a large working-class membership was the idea of saving a small sum each week to ensure a respectable funeral. Quite what constituted a respectable funeral was, of course, likely to be a matter for some debate. Neil Munro's kirk beadle and waiter, Erchie, a man who knew a thing or two about funerals by virtue of his two professions, found this out when his neighbour, big Macphee, was buried and the deceased's country relatives complained about the lack of style of a Glasgow funeral:

> There wasna a sowl that left this close behind the corp today had crape in his hat except my ain man. . . . And there was anither thing; I didna expect to see onybody else but my man in weepers, him bein' the only freen' puir Macphee had but – . . . Whit's mair my man was the only wan there wi' a dacent shirt wi' tucks on the breist o't; the rest o' ye had that sma' respect for the deid ye went wi' shirt-breists as flet as a sheet o' paper. It was showin' awfu' sma' respect for puir Macphee.

Erchie explains patiently that black crepe, mourning bands and dress shirts were no longer *de rigeur* at Glasgow funerals, however much they might still be the fashion in rural Fintry:

> Oot Fintry way, it's a' richt to keep up tucked shirt-breists, and crape, and weepers, and mort-cloths, and the like, for there cann be an awfu' lot o' gaiety in the place, but we have aye plenty o' ither things to amuse us in Gleska. There's the Kelvingrove Museum, and the Waxworks.

Appropriate catering at funerals was another serious issue. Elsewhere, Erchie tells how he had in the course of his waiting career:

> . . .handed roond seed-cake and a wee drap o' spirits at a burial, wi' a bereaved and mournfu' mainner that greatly consoled the weedow.

However comforting Erchie's seed-cake may have been,

the essential dish at the post-funeral reception was, of course, boiled ham.

Death runs through the Scottish imagination, surfacing most obviously in literature, but also informing our political thought. The framers of the American constitution spoke memorably of man's inalienable rights to "life, liberty and the pursuit of happiness" – it is surely not without significance that the authors of the Declaration of Arbroath, while covering the same area did so with a characteristically Scottish flavour:

> For so long as one hundred men remain alive, we shall
> never under any conditions submit to the domination
> of the English. It is not for glory or riches or honours
> that we fight, but only for liberty, which no good man
> will consent to lose but with his life.

The tangled tale of Scotland's religious obsession is dealt with in "A peculiar people" but a chapter entitled "Old Mortality" can hardly avoid looking at the impact of religious martyrdom on the Scottish spirit. After all, a nation which can find as euphonious a euphemism for violent death as "To Glorify God in the Grassmarket" and in which to this day earnest souls record and restore the graves of the Covenanting martyrs, surely has a special feel for death.

Even such a rebel against the Calvinist certainties of his personal and national background as Robert Louis Stevenson felt the pull of the dead of the seventeenth century wars of religion. His first published work was an adolescent account of the Battle of Rullion Green, while one of his finest and most moving poems (albeit written from the distance-lent enchantment of the Pacific) celebrates the hill places where the Covenanter dead lie:

> Blows the wind to-day, and the sun and the rain are
>   flying,

Blows the wind on the moors to-day and now,
Where about the graves of the martyrs the whaups are
 crying.
My heart remembers how. . .

The grip that the death of the Covenanters has had on
generations of Scots is testified to in works like Walter
Scott's *Old Mortality* and John Galt's *Ringan Ghilhaize*.

Scotland's literary death-fixation has however deeper
and older roots than the "Killing Times". Perhaps the
most frequently anthologised poem of, arguably, our
greatest poet of the early modern period – William
Dunbar (*c*.1465 – *c*.1513) is that litany to death – *The
Lament for the Makaris* :

> Our plesance heir is all vane glory,
> This fals world is bot transitory,
> The flesche is brukle, the Fend is sle;
> *Timor mortis conturbat me*
>
> On to the ded gois all Estatis,
> Princis, Prelotis, and Potestatis,
> Baith riche and pur of al degre;
> *Timor mortis conturbat me.*

The *Lament*, with its doleful list of the poets and
scholars carried of by the dread hand of death was
not, of course, Dunbar's only death-inspired poem – his
Elegy on the death of Bernard Stewart, Lord of Aubigny
rings out aliteratively:

> O duilfull death! O dragon dolorous!
> Why hes thow done so dulfullie devoir
> The prince of knychtheid, nobill and chivilrous,
> The witt of weiris, of armes and honour,
> The crop of curage, the frength of armes in stour. . .

Dunbar's poems are in the tradition of the royal courts
and of high art – closer to the folk tradition are the

Scottish Ballads – and a more blood-soaked, death-obsessed body of literature it would be hard to find. Consider the *Twa Corbies* with its cynical and gruesome account of the plans of two crows to dispose of the body of "a new-slain knight":

> His hound is to the hunting gane,
> His hawk to fetch the wild fowl hame
> His lady has ta'en another mate,
> Sae we may mak' our denner sweet.

> Ye'll sit on his white hause-bane,
> And I'll pike out his bonny blue een,
> Wi' ae lock o' his gowden hair
> We'll theek our nest when it grows bare. . .

Or the patricidal tale of *Edward* who tells his mother

> O I hae killed my fader dear, mither, mither;
> O I hae killed my fader dear,
> Alas and wae is me

but we learn by the end of the poem

> The curse of hell frae me sall ye bear, mither, mither;
> The curse of hell frae me sall ye bear,
> Sic counsels ye gave to me O.

Even a less ghoulish ballad like *Sir Patrick Spens* quickly moves from the calm opening of the king in Dunfermline "drinking the blude-reid wine" through Sir Patrick's cry of anguish

> O wha is this has don this deid,
> This ill deid don to me,
> To send me out this time o' the yeir,
> To sail upon the sea

to the inevitably tragic end

> Haf owre, haf owre to Aberdour,
> It's fiftie fadom deip,

And thair lies guid Sir Patrick Spens
Wi' the Scots lords at his feit.

With such a heritage, is it any wonder that Scottish writers have found in death a fruitful source of inspiration. Death is likely to come in, almost unbidden, into any Scottish writing from Lady Nairne's *Caller Herrin'*, where the vendor sings:

Wha'll buy my caller herrin'?
Oh, ye may ca' them vulgar farin' –
Wives and mithers, maist despairin',
Ca' them lives o' men. . .

to Stevenson's *Weir of Hermiston*.

RLS had the advantage of a childhood brought up on the bloodier tales of the Covenanters and, doubtless not unconnected, a life-long predisposition, manifested in works like *Jekyll and Hyde* and *The Bodysnatchers*, towards the dark and the macabre. *Weir of Hermiston* opens with a dispute between Archie Weir and his father, the Lord Justice-Clerk, Lord Hermiston, over the death of a convicted criminal – a dispute summed up by Hermiston as:

You're a young gentleman that doesna approve of Capital Punishment. . . weel, I'm an auld man that does. I was glad to get Jopp hangit, and for what would I pretend I wasna.

Stevenson, whose family home housed a piece of furniture allegedly made by the famous, or infamous, Deacon Brodie, would doubtless have enjoyed the tale of Brodie, before his exectution, saying to an Edinburgh magistrate:

Fare ye weel, Baillie! Ye needna be surprised if ye see me amang ye yet, to take my share o' the Deid Chack.

The Deid Chack was a celebratory meal, indulged in by the city officials, after attending an execution.

Executions, and indeed murders, have provided some of the most vivid episodes in the popular history, iconography and demonology of Scotland. Is there a better known woman in Victorian Scotland than Madeleine Smith, the genteel poisoner of Blythswood Square, Glasgow? Was there a finer example of judicial murder than the execution of the crew of the English ship *Worcester* in 1705, and were the bloody propensities of the Edinburgh mob ever shown to better effect than in the lynching of Captain Porteous in 1736?

If the mob was violent, the old Scots judiciary was no less given to what seems at times to have been a death obsession. Lord Braxfield, on whom Stevenson modelled his judge in *Weir of Hermiston*, is still remembered for his comment to a prisoner before him:

> Ye're a vera clever chiel, man, but ye wad be none the
> waur o' a hanging

Equally famous is his retort to the radical reformer Joseph Gerrald, who had had the temerity to remind Braxfield that Christ himself was a reformer:

> Muckle he made o' that, he was hangit

and just to prove the consistency of Braxfield's views we have his maxim:

> Hang a thief when he is young, and he'll no steal
> when he is auld.

Twentieth century Scotland has not turned her back on her obsession with death – poets still write of death – sometimes movingly, sometimes pretentiously

> A Scottish poet maun assume
> The burden o' his people's doom,
> And dee to brak' their livin tomb
>   Hugh MacDiarmid, *A Drunk Man Looks at the Thistle*

Scottish novelists still find in death and the contemplation of the last things fruitful sources of inspiration. In John Buchan's last novel, *Sick Heart River*, the hero, Sir Edward Leithen, aware of his impending death from tuberculosis reflects:

> . . . how was he to spend his closing months? As an invalid, slowly growing feebler, always expectant of death? That was starkly impossible. He wanted peace to make his soul, but not lethargy either of mind or body.

The idea of the hero making his soul, of a good death, is a recurring theme in Buchan's works. In *Greenmantle*, Richard Hannay, Blenkiron and Sandy Arbuthnot are trapped and facing certain death. Sandy tells his friends:

> We're lucky fellows. . . we've all had our whack. When I remember the good times I've had I could sing a hymn of praise. We've lived long enough to know ourselves, and to shape ourselves into some kind of decency.

The literary death fascination continues. In James Kennaway's 1950's novel *Tunes of Glory* the ex-ranker and acting C.O., Jock Sinclair, having driven the new and unpopular Commanding Officer to suicide, arranges a spectacularly elaborate military funeral of the type normally reserved for national heroes:

> The death they say is a victory. The death they say's the great triumph. We'll march away to the "Black Bear". The "Black Bear's" to pull us together. . . All the tunes of glory! We'll have them all, to remember the more clearly. We'll have all the tunes of glory!. . . It'll be a right funeral, I know it will. It's as I said. I've seen it once already. And it'll be the least we can do.

It may be argued that what we have described as a death obsession is not unique to the Scots and that death is, after all, one of the great universal themes and that it is hardly likely that Scots would have ignored a subject which has so memorably engaged the world's greatest writers and thinkers. However enough outside observers have remarked on this trait in the Scottish character to suggest that there is evidence for a specially Scottish concern with death. Wallace Notestein, the American historian, in his *The Scot in History* is talking of the Scot's sense of humour when he says:

> He has an incredible number of stories about death and funerals. Death has always interested him and funerals have been one of his diversions.

An interest, by the way, which finds expression in a remarkable number of memorable monumental inscriptions – from the sadly apocryphal:

> Here lie the bones of Elizabeth Charlotte
> That was born a virgin and died a harlot
> She was aye a virgin till seventeen –
> An extraordinary thing for Aberdeen

to the better attested Fife inscription:

> In this churchyard lies Eppie Coutts
> Either here, or hereabouts:
> But where it is, none can tell
> Till Eppie rise and tell hersel'

through the gritty Coatbridge realism of:

> Here lies the body of Georgie Denham
> If ye saw him now ye wadna ken him

to what might be interpreted as a typically Aberdonian interest in establishing a sensible and business-like relationship with the Almighty – a concern elegantly expressed in the much quoted lines:

Here lies Martin Elginbrod
Have mercy on my soul, Lord God,
As I would do were I Lord God,
And Thou were Martin Elginbrod

Where such a fascination, amounting to an obsession, with death comes from is clearly a debatable matter, the full exploration of which would take us beyond the limits of the present work. However, it is fairly clear that the religious and social forces unleashed by the Reformation and the Wars of Religion had their effects on what, from the mediaeval evidence, would seem to have been an innate predisposition towards a interest in death. John Buchan, writing of the Covenanters in his *Montrose* argues:

> They must be judged by their work, and beyond
> doubt they gave to the Scottish people a moral
> seriousness, a conception of the deeper issues of life,
> and an intellectual *ascesis* gifts which may well atone
> for their many infirmities.

Education is, of course, another Scotch Obsession and will be dealt with elsewhere, but it is reasonable to note here that the view of the Scottish peasantry as the most literate example of that class in Europe, has its implications for our thoughts on death. The object of literacy was the establishment of the Godly Commonwealth and schools were established for the advancement of "civilitie, godlines, knowledge and learning". The literate masses found themselves presented with little reading material by way of diversion from the Scripture, works of devotion and accounts of martyrs and the tribulations of the church. Is it to be wondered that a diet of such works – which by their very nature tended towards a concentration on death and eschatology – should develop the national taste for such profundities?

It is indeed, perhaps, more remarkable that with such a solemn, not to say costive, diet the black humour of death should still shine through – as in the old Dumbartonshire story of the Laird of Garscadden. Garscadden and some fellow landowners had been drinking hard all night when the unnaturally pale appearance of Garscadden was noted:

> Garscadden looks unco gash

observed one of the more perceptive (or more sober) of his companions to their host, who replied:

> Deil mend him! He's been wi' his maker these last twa hoors. I saw him slip awa' but I didna' like to disturb good company by saying aught aboot it.

JOCK TAMSON'S BAIRNS

The Scots and Democracy

There can surely be no more potent and prevailing Scotch obsession than democracy. An almost mystical belief in the Scottish democratic tradition is to be found playing a vital part in the thinking of politicians of all shades of opinion. The Left builds on the notion of a traditional Scottish commitment to democracy and freedom and cites exemplars from Calgacus through Wallace to the Poll Tax campaigners. The Right takes from the supposedly democratic structure of an older paternalistic society a justification for a system of relationships sympathetic to its creeds. Remarkably enough the same phenomenon can conveniently provide both right and left with evidence for their beliefs – the democratic kinship of the clan system can, for example, be enthusiastically defended by landed aristocrats and the 1920's communist propagandist John MacLean:

> The Communism of the clans must be re-established
> on a modern basis. . .

Truly this Scottish democracy is a most remarkable thing. But does it actually exist in any historical context?

In its most simple definition democracy is government by the people and as such is a recent Scottish phenomenon. Before the passing of the 1832 Reform Act political power in Scotland – as measured by the right to vote for Members of Parliament – was limited to around 5,000 people. The Reform Act increased this to around 60,000 male voters at a time when the total male population of Scotland was 1.1 million. On any reasonable measure "democracy" in Scotland could not be said to have arrived until the advent of universal adult suffrage in 1928.

But this is too simple a definition – there undoubtedly is and was within Scotland something which could be recognised and which could conveniently be labelled a democratic tendency. Whatever this was, it rather strangely combined at one and the same time a regard for individual worth and a strong collectivist sentiment. There runs through Scottish history and culture a concern for Jock Tamson, or in the language of Sir David Lyndsay's *Satire of the Three Estates* – John Commonweal. There is a widely held view that:

> The rank is but the guinea's stamp
> The man's the gowd for a' that

However it is quite a long step from recognising that "a man's a man for a' that" to agreeing that the man should share in political power.

The democratic obsession of Scotland has perhaps two main sources. One has already been alluded to in MacLean's comment on the "Communism of the clans", the other is to be found in the more lowland culture of the "kailyard" and the concept of the opportunities for boot-strap advancement open to the "lad o' pairts". Both these sources are, however, deeply flawed as the founts of democracy.

The clan system was far from democratic; at its best it may perhaps have been collectivist. However when chiefs like the Earl of Mar of the '15 wrote to his factor:

> . . . let my own tenants in Kildrummie know, that if
> they come not forth with their best arms, I will send
> immediately a party to burn what they shall miss
> taking from them. . .

or "gentle Lochiel" of the '45 declared his support for
the Jacobite rising in these terms:

> I'll share the fate of my Prince and so shall every man
> over whom nature or fortune has given me any power.

we can hardly claim the clan system placed chief and
clansman on a footing of political equality. What the
old order did have was a sense of mutual obligation, a
relationship of service and protection which was not
based on what Thomas Carlyle described as the cash
nexus. The clan system was paternalistic – the very word
clan derives from the Gaelic *clann*, meaning children,
but at least it saw the chief's followers as more than units
of production or serfs bound to the soil. The survival of
servile status among lowland colliers until the late eighteenth century does serve as a warning not to make too
great claims for the universality of Scottish democracy.

Equally fallacious is the view that the opportunity
for advancement offered to the idealised "lad o' pairts"
was in any real sense a democratic force. That it was
possible for the "lad o' pairts" from a village school to
advance in society is not disputed – that enough did so
to be seen as any sort of democratic force did so must be
questioned. Even more questionable is the view that
such a social advance for the individual need in any way
represent anything of a democratic gain for society. The
possibility of upward social movement did exist, but the
process was one of absorption into the landed society,
and usually an acceptance of the values of that society.

The dominance of Scottish political, administrative,
cultural and learned society by the landed classes

through most of our history was all but total. To take one example of this dominance we may turn to poetry. The praise that was heaped on Burns as a "ploughman poet" reflects the fact that most of his predecessors in the Scottish canon were from a different social strata – Barbour, a cleric; Dunbar, a courtier, probably related to the Earls of Dunbar; Kennedy, a younger son of Lord Kennedy of Dunure; Drummond, a courtier and Midlothian landowner; David Lyndsay, Fife landowner and Lord Lyon King of Arms.

The case of Robert McQueen, Lord Braxfield, Lord Justice-Clerk of Scotland from 1788 – 1799, and hardly one of the greatest advocates of democratic sentiment, is instructive in this context. MacQueen's grandfather had been a gardener on a landed estate, the gardener's son had by the "lad o' pairts" route got a good education, became factor to the Earl of Selkirk's Lanarkshire estates and married into the local gentry. His son Robert, educated at Lanark Grammar School and Edinburgh University, was admitted to the Faculty of Advocates in 1744. Once on the judicial bench, however, Braxfield was a determined and indeed vicious opponent of democratic activists such as Muir, Skirving and Margarot.

It is interesting to compare Braxfield and perhaps his most distinguished victim, Thomas Muir of Huntershill. Muir was, like Braxfield, a small land owner. Muir, was, like Braxfield, a member of the Faculty of Advocates. Both Muir's and Braxfield's families had been established in similar social and professional ranks for much the same length of time. Muir had, however, been involved in democratic activism, perhaps the more dangerous in Braxfield's view because Muir's activism had been among the working classes. Braxfield summed up at Muir's trial for sedition:

A Government in every country should be just like a
corporation; and in this country, it is made up of the
landed interest, which alone has the right to be
represented. As for the rabble, who have nothing but
personal property, what hold has the nation on them?

Muir's comment was:

I have devoted myself to the cause of the people.
It is a good cause – it shall ultimately prevail.

The "lad o' pairts" route for Robert MacQueen does
not seem to have brought in its train much democratic
sentiment, whatever other intellectual and moral
qualities it might be justly possible to credit Braxfield
with.

If we cannot find much democracy in Scotland then
can we find some other force, and account for the
strength of this obsession?

Perhaps it is the idea of individual worth and
individual responsibility and a right to freedom that
is closer to the "We're all Jock Tamson's bairns"
notion than any concept of all Jock Tamson's bairns
having equal rights and sharing in political power;
individualism, however, of a particularly Scottish
type, an individualism mediated by a collectivist social
contract. One of the totemic Scottish texts is the
Declaration of Arbroath. While this is far from being a
"democratic" document in a narrow or technical sense
of that word, subscribed as it was by a small elite group
drawn from the nobility and higher clergy of 1320s
Scotland, it does speak in the name of:

the rest of the barons and freeholders, and whole
community, of the kingdom of Scotland

and this reference to what has otherwise been expressed
as the "community of the realm" is very significant.

When William Wallace emerged in the 1290s from the obscurity of being a small laird's younger son to lead the patriotic forces, he did so as "Guardian of Scotland", deriving his power and authority from this community of the realm. The *Declaration*, in a remarkable passage for a document emanating from a fourteenth-century feudal state, declares that if King Robert:

> the person who hath restored the people's safety in defence of their liberties.

should attempt to subvert these liberties:

> we will immediately endeavour to expel him, as our enemy and as the subverter both of his and our rights, and we will make another king, who will defend our liberties.

This is heady stuff, far headier and far more significant in fact than the more famous passage which immediately follows:

> For so long as there shall but one hundred of us remain alive we will never give consent to subject ourselves to the dominion of the English. For it is not glory, it is not riches, neither is it honours, but it is liberty alone that we fight and contend for, which no honest man will lose but with his life.

The second passage is a noble hymn to national liberty but could arguably be written, *mutatis mutandis*, by any people at any time. The first passage, with its clearly stated social contract between king and people, with its fiercely conditional loyalty to the King, would be a remarkable statement at any time. It is the more remarkable in its origins in a country which had just won back its freedom and territorial integrity after years of bloody struggle and sacrifice under the inspirational leadership of this same King who is threatened with expulsion for hypothetical backsliding in the national cause.

In John Barbour's epic poem *The Bruce*, written around the end of the fourteenth-century, we find some striking source material for the Scottish belief in the rights of the community to enjoy freedom:

> A! Fredome is a noble thing!
> Fredome mays man to haiff liking;
> Fredome all solace to man giffis:
> He levys at es that frely levys

and later Barbour has the King addressing his army before Bannockburn:

> . . .we haf the richt;
> And for the richt ilk man suld ficht.

> . . .that we for our lyvis
> And for our childer and our wifis,
> And for the fredome of our land,
> Ar strenyeit in battale for to stand

Bruce, the hero-King leading a national struggle for freedom; and Wallace, the common man raised to be the protector of his people as Guardian of Scotland, are powerful images in the creation of national myth or national identity. The unity of the nation forged in the Wars of Independence and proved at Bannockburn depended on the involvement of both rulers and ruled and implies a positive relationship between the various orders of society.

It is no accident of semantics that the title of the King was "King of Scots", not, "King of Scotland". The concept of a greater entity, of an over-arching sense of nationhood, that could not be contained or limited in the person of the King is implicit both in the *Declaration* and in this title of "King of Scots" and is perhaps the most genuine part of the Scotch obsession with democracy.

It would be anachronistic to believe that this meant that power rested with the people, the masses, but authority and the roots of authority were clearly to be found in the "community of the realm". This fourteenth-century "community of the realm" may not, in effect, have been much wider a political community than that which was implied by Lord Braxfield's eighteenth-century dictum:

> Government in every country should be just like a corporation; and in this country, it is made up of the landed interest. . .

Even so the remarkable degree of incorporation of a large part of the population into the political class which legitimated government, even if it did not actively take part in government itself, is noteworthy. Once the concept of absolutism, of all power descending from God through the King and down the feudal chain, is removed then there is a new force present. This new force is the doctrine of government by the consent of the people, and the possibility of a limitation on the power of the ruler, whether that ruler be King or Parliament. An interesting and forceful expression of this concept came in 1953 in Lord Cooper's judgement in the case *MacCormick v Lord Advocate* which was brought to question the legality within Scotland of the Queen's style as "Elizabeth II". Lord Cooper, the Lord President of the Court of Session, observed:

> The principle of the unlimited sovereignty of Parliament is a distinctively English principle which has no counterpart in Scottish constitutional law.

The connection between Scottish democratic sentiment and the Presbyterian system of church government has frequently been commented on. If one is to accept the *Declaration of Arbroath* and the concept of the "community of the realm" as being, if not democratic concepts, at least proto-democratic or consensual rather than hierarchical then obviously such sentiments pre-date Presbyterianism by two and half centuries and Presbyterianism as such cannot be seen as a source for Scottish democracy. It still remains possible to argue that reformed church government, with its emphasis on egalitarian concepts such as the right of congregations to call their own pastor, the priesthood of all believers, equality of clergy, the ordination of lay elders, vernacular Scripture, poor relief, reinforced the democratic and collectivist tendencies in Scotland. It is also equally possible to argue that such a system of church government proved popular in Scotland because it was in harmony with an existing strand in the national character. The following extracts from the *First Book of Discipline* which set out the constitution and structure of the reformed Church are indicative of this Scottish cast of mind:

> It appertaineth to the people, and to every several congregation, to elect their Minister. . .

> . . .for the widow and fatherless, the aged, impotent, or lamed, who neither can nor may travail for their sustentation, we say that God commandeth his people to be careful. . .

> Men of best knowledge in God's word, of cleanest life, men faithful, and of most honest conversation that can be found in the Church, must be nominated to be in election. . . The election of Elders and Deacons ought to be used every year once. . . lest that by long continuance of such officers, men presume upon the liberty of the Church. . .

> We think it a thing most expedient and necessary, that every Church have a Bible in English, and that the

people be commanded to convene to hear the plain
reading or interpretation of the Scripture. . .

If the Scottish people had no democratic control over
their destiny until this century, this does not mean that
they had no democratic input into their destiny or
lacked any means of influencing events. There was
always the "Jenny Geddes" approach to political
debate, where a skilfully thrown missile substituted
for the ballot box. The power of the Edinburgh mob
was felt on a number of occasions in the nation's history
and the wider Scottish record of meal riots and anti-
militia riots demonstrates the activist tendency of the
unenfranchised part of the population. This populist
involvement in the political process was well summed
up by Walter Scott, in the words he gave to Mr
Plumdamas and Mrs Howden in *The Heart of Midlothian*.
Mrs Howden and her neighbours in post-Union
Edinburgh are discussing the reprieve of Captain
Porteous who had, as Captain of the City Guard, fired
on a crowd attempting to free a popular smuggler,
Andrew Wilson, from the gallows:

> "I am judging," said Mr Plumdamas, "that this
> reprieve wadna stand gude in the auld Scots law,
> when the kingdom *was* a kingdom."
>   "I dinna ken muckle about the law," answered
> Mrs Howden; "but I ken, when we had a king, and a
> chancellor, and parliament-men o' our ain, we could
> aye peeble them wi' stones when they werena gude
> bairns – But naebody's nails can reach the length
> o' Lunnon."

Thirty years earlier, when the Scottish parliament was
debating the Treaty of Union, Lord Belhaven, in a
famous speech, foresaw the impact of Union on what,
although he did not use those terms, he clearly

envisaged as the "community of the realm." His list of components in this community included:

> a free and independent Kingdom
> a National Church
> the Noble and Honourable Peerage of Scotland
> the Honourable Estate of Barons
> the Royal State of Burrows
> our Learned Judges
> the Valliant and Gallant Soldiery
> the Honest Industrious Tradesman
> the Laborious Plew-man
> the Landedmen
> our Mariners

Belhaven was certainly not suggesting that the last five categories should be incorporated into the political establishment, but what he surely was suggesting was that the state was a collectivity which had to take some account of the needs and wishes of "the Honest Industrious Tradesmen" as well as of "the Noble and Honourable Peerage of Scotland". Belhaven was hardly a leveller, his categorisation of the "community of the realm" is inherently and inevitably hierarchical and class-ridden; but it is also possible to see it as inherently Scottish in its recognition of the worth and individuality of all the component parts of the community.

It is perhaps not quite as great a leap as might be thought from Belhaven to Burns. Belhaven expressed a view on the problems and values of all parts of the social matrix; Burns reminds us that worth does not reside in only one part of this social matrix:

> A prince can mak a belted knight,
> A marquis, duke an' a' that!
> But an honest man's aboon his might -
> Guid faith, he mauna' fa' that
> For a' that, an' a' that,

Their dignities, an a' that,
The pith o' sense an' pride o' worth
Are higher rank than a' that.

Burns has brought the democratic debate into recognisably modern terms. In modern times Scotland's self-image has been strongly democratic. In British terms the Scottish contribution to the development of popular and democratic politics has been considerable. From the Chartists of the 1840s through the early trade unions, the formation of the Labour Party and the Independent Labour Party, the impression that Scotland has made on the rest of the United Kingdom has been of a progressive, left of centre, democratic and collectivist society.

Scots have even managed to believe this themselves – often in the face of quite persuasive contrary evidence – this, of course, is the mark of a true obsession! The memory of Keir Hardie and Red Clydeside notwithstanding, the only political party this century ever to win an absolute majority of the popular vote in Scotland at a General Election was the Conservative Party in 1955. Admittedly this election took place in what was virtually a two-party environment and the result was aided by the low-water mark of contemporary Liberalism, but nevertheless it serves as a significant corrective to a facile attribution of democratic tendencies to only one political party or to an assumption that Scotland is now an inherently socialist or leftist nation.

Stands Scotland where it did?

asked Macduff in *Macbeth* – and perhaps the same question could be asked of contemporary Scotland and her pretensions to democracy. The achievement of universal suffrage has answered the question in one sense. In another there is still a view at large in Scotland that the nation is in some way different in its approach to democracy and politics – "we're all Jock Tamson's bairns" is still a powerful and influential concept. Scots happily attribute to themselves a more egalitarian spirit, a greater commitment to collectivism, a higher sense of community than they attribute to others, and specifically to the English.

One of the touchstones of this differentiation was to be found during the Premiership of Margaret Thatcher (1979-1990). The emphasis placed by her administration on individualism as opposed to community, on "family values" as opposed to corporate action, on non-intervention in the economy, was perceived to be at odds with the Scottish cast of mind and the Scottish political consensus. There had, for example, been cross-party commitment in Scotland to supporting key elements in the industrial fabric of the nation. The Thatcherite refusal to support these alleged "lame-ducks" in ship-building, steel-making, heavy engineering, broke with this tradition. The declining electoral support for Conservatism in Scotland was adduced as evidence for a fundamental incompatibility between the socially sensitive communitarian and collectivist tendencies of Scotland and the individualism of Thatcherite Conservatism. The growth of support for this brand of Conservatism among the southern English working-classes – the group characterised as "Essex Man" – was similarly presented, particularly in Nationalist circles, as evidence of a substantial and widening Anglo-Scottish political and cultural gulf. Conservative politicians from the Premier downwards , who presented their version of the economics of Adam Smith and cited traditional Scottish principles of economy and thrift as reinforcements to their arguments, were surprised and disappointed to find their policies and candidates rejected and Scots thirled to what English tabloid commentators characterised as a "dependency culture".

One of the defining moments in this mutual incomprehension came in 1988 when Mrs Thatcher addressed the General Assembly of the Church of Scotland. Her somewhat anti-climactic speech emphasised personal and family responsibility and was widely criticised for its neglect of a sense of a wider community. The Kirk was perhaps the wrong audience for such an address – if, in earlier years, the Church of England had been described as "the Tory Party at prayer", many might have been tempted to describe the Church of Scotland of the 70s and 80s as the Labour Party at prayer. A socially radical strand had of course been apparent in Scottish Presbyterianism for centuries, emerging on issues like the Disruption of 1843 and showing itself in manifestations such as George MacLeod's Iona Community and the leftward leaning, unilateralist, anti-apartheid General Assemblies of this period followed to the full in this tradition.

Perhaps the jury, inevitably, is still out on this Scotch Obsession. Whether or not Scots are more democratic and freedom-loving and caring and egalitarian than anyone else is a moot point and not, perhaps, for a Scot to judge. However there are worse aspirations.

> For a' that an' a' that
> It's comin yet for a' that,
> That Man to Man the warld o'er,
> Shall brothers be for a' that.

THE WATER OF LIFE

The Scots and Drink

*I*f ever a nation was defined by its national drink then that nation is Scotland – all round the world the call for a "Scotch" is a clearly understood shorthand term for Scotland's most famous product – whisky. The word whisky is, of course, simply a corruption of the Gaelic *uisge beatha*, the water of life – a term analogous to the French generic term for distilled spirits – *eau de vie*. For over 500 years – so far as the written record runs – Scotland has been producing this distinctive spirit from the distillation of malted grain. Friar John Cor appears in the Scottish Exchequer Roll in 1494 as receiving eight bolls of malt to make *aqua vitae* – again the water of life, this time in Latin. However certainly this entry may mark the start of the formal record it is inconceivable that the history of distillation in Scotland is not considerably older. There are indeed those misguided souls who would claim that the secret was brought from Ireland – but these are the same sort of people who claim that the Dutch invented golf and should be treated with sympathetic contempt.

Whisky has been so much a part of Scotland and the Scotch imagination, that the attempts to regularise and legitimise the distilling of whisky by issuing licences met with considerable resistance. It is said that George

Smith of Glenlivet, the first man to take out a Government licence in 1824, was so unpopular with his neighbours for his surrender to legitimacy that he had to carry a pair of pistols with him for protection.

Not only Scots, but generations of visitors to Scotland, have had a fascination with whisky. Dr Samuel Johnson, by no means an enthusiast for things Scottish, when on his 1773 tour of the Highlands, cried to his travelling companion James Boswell:

> Come, let me know what it is makes a Scotchman happy!

and ordered a gill of whisky from the Inn at Inveraray. This he tells us was the only time he sampled it and the Doctor reports thus on the experiment:

> . . .I thought it preferable to any English malt brandy. It was strong, but not pungent, and was free from the empyreumatik taste or smell. What was the process I had not opportunity of inquiring, nor do I wish to improve the art of making poison pleasant.

Not, perhaps, the most glowing endorsement – one can hardly see The Macallan advertising itself as "free from the empyreumatik taste" – the word simply means burnt.

King George IV in 1822 demanded, as part of his Walter Scott stage-managed immersion in all things Scottish, Glenlivet whisky. This proved to be difficult to obtain in Edinburgh and Mrs Grant of Rothiemurchus tells in her *Memoirs of a Highland Lady* how her father instructed her to :

> . . .empty my pet bin, where was whiskey long in wood, long in uncorked bottles, mild as milk, and the true contraband *goût* in it. Much as I grudged this treasure it made our fortunes afterwards . . .

One can perhaps see more than a touch of Scotch Obsession in Mrs Grant's reluctance to share her illicitly distilled stock even with the King, although as she says her father's later appointment to an Indian Judgeship was due to his surrender of the whisky stock.

The superiority of Glenlivet and the antiquity of whisky distilling are entertainingly attested to in the comic poem by the nineteenth-century Scottish novelist and poet, W. E. Aytoun, *The Massacre of the MacPherson* , which goes on to relate how:

Fhairson had a son,
Who married Noah's daughter
And nearly spoil'd ta Flood,
By trinking up ta water:
Which he would have done
I at least believe it,
Had ta mixture peen
Only half Glenlivet.

Views on the benefits of whisky have been varied – and held with passion. Neil Munro's puffer skipper Para Handy was known to speak of the merits of:

Wholesome Brutish spirits

and Burns clearly had no doubts about the curative power of one of the most famous Highland whiskies – Ferintosh – distilled on the estate of Forbes of Culloden, but banned under excise regulations:

Thee, Ferintosh! O sadly lost!
Scotland lament frae coast to coast!
Now colic-grips, an' barkin hoast,
May kill us a';
For loyal Forbes' Charter'd boast
Is taen awa!

A more extreme expression of belief in whisky's powers

was given by James Hogg, the "Ettrick Shepherd", who wrote:

> If a body could find out the exac' proper proportion and quantity that ought to be drunk and keep to that, I verily trow that he might leeve forever and never die at a', and that doctors and kirkyards would go oot o' fashion

Another Scottish writer who knew his whisky, Tobias Smollett, recorded in *Humphry Clinker* that:

> The Highlanders. . . regale themselves with whisky, a malt spirit; as strong as geneva, which they swallow in great quantities, without any signs of inebriation: they are used to it from the cradle, and find it an excellent preservative against the winter cold, which must be extreme on these mountains – I am told that it is given with great success to infants, as a cordial, in the confluent smallpox, when the eruption seems to flag, and the symptoms grow unfavourable.

Smollett, it is appropriate to note, had been a surgeon in the Royal Navy and later was in medical practice in London, but clearly had not lost his innate belief in the virtues of whisky. Quite apart from the national faith these extracts have demonstrated in whisky as restorative, panacea and specific for smallpox in infancy, there is another dimension to the national obsession, a dimension summed up in Burns' cry:

> Freedom and Whisky gang thegither

Whisky has been seen as an expression of national identity; the absence of whisky as an offence to a Scot's nature and self-esteem. Compton MacKenzie's novel *Whisky Galore*, set in wartime whisky-rationed Hebridean islands, the aptly named Great and Little Todday, has a cargo of whisky, bound for the USA as part of the wartime export drive, cast up by shipwreck

just in time to allow George Campbell to get enough
Dutch courage to tell his dragon of a mother that he
intends to marry. The providential arrival also allows
the Doctor to make good his promise to the old and
dying crofter Hector MacRurie:

> Whisky will come again and the sun will shine again . . .
> and you and I are going to look each other in the eyes,
> the two old friends that we are, and I can hear the words
> chiming in my mind like a noble peal of bells. *Slàinte
> mhath, slàinte mhór*. And then the two of us are going to
> drain our glasses to the last golden heart-warming drop.

While whisky was the indigenous spirit of the
Highlands and since the nineteenth century the entire
nation's spirit of choice, earlier generations in the
Lowlands were brandy drinkers; a testament to the
centuries of commercial, cultural and political inter-
change with France – a relationship formalised by,
but not limited to, the Auld Alliance.

The French connection also meant that Scotland was
a major importer of French wine – in particular the
red wines of Bordeaux. The strength of this trade is
suggested in John Home's lines inspired by the post-
Union adoption of trade preference for England's oldest
ally, Portugal:

> Bold and erect the Caledonian stood,
> Old was his mutton and his claret good;
> 'Let him drink port', the English statesman cried –
> He drank the poison, and his spirit died.

Indeed the enthusiasm of the Scots for wine has been
well attested, from Burns calling for generous quantities:

> Go fetch to me a pint o' wine,
> And fill it in a silver tassie;
> That I may drink, before I go,
> A service to my bonnie lassie

to the remarkable drinking habits of the Scottish judges of the eighteenth-century, who normally presided at trials with a bottle on the bench before them. One of these judicial, if not judicious, drinkers, Lord Hermand, sums up a very Scottish attitude to drink. An advocate had been pleading before Hermand that his client's sentence should be mitigated because he was drunk at the time the offence had been committed – an appeal His Lordship rejected with some contempt:

> . . .if he did this when he was drunk what would he not do when he's sober?

Hermand was a serious drinker. His younger contemporary, Lord Cockburn, wrote of him:

> With Hermand drinking was a virtue; he had a serious respect for drinking, indeed a high moral approbation, and a serious compassion for the poor wretches who could not indulge in it, and with due contempt of those who could but did not.

The approving words "he can take a good dram" is still heard today and the Hermand view, or a cruder version of it, which identifies a capacity for drink with manliness and virtue, is undoubtedly a prevailing Scottish attitude. Jock Sinclair, in James Kennaway's *Tunes of Glory,* is in his element at an Officer's Mess party and orders drinks for everyone:

> Whisky. For the gentlemen that like it and for the gentlemen who don't like it, whisky.

Later, he questions one of the regimental pipers about his state of sobriety and warns the piper:

> You're no here to get sick drunk the same as the rest of us are

Jock Sinclair's view has not, of course, won universal

acceptance in Scotland. A national obsession with drink has manifested itself in two modes – what might be called the Tam o' Shanter approach:

> Tam had got planted unco right;
> Fast by an ingle, bleezing finely,
> Wi' reaming swats, that drank divinely
> And at his elbow, Souter Johnny,
> His ancient, trusty, drouthy crony;
> Tam lo'ed him like a vera brither;
> They had been fou for weeks thegither. . .

and the Kate approach:

> O Tam! hadst thou but been sae wise,
> As ta'en thy ain wife Kate's advice!
> She tauld thee weel thou was a skellum,
> A blethering, blustering, drunken blellum. . .

The fabric of the nation has been as much affected by the temperance movement – generations were brought up in one of the many organisations such as the Rechabites, the Good Templars, and the Band of Hope. The regulation of drinking law in the nineteenth century by measures such as the Forbes Mackenzie Act – the Public Houses (Scotland) Act of 1853 – which introduced the novelty of an official closing time and also closed the public houses altogether on Sundays. The exception to this was an exemption for hotels which could stay open to serve a category of clients known as *bona fide* travellers. A consequence of this was a remarkable need which many people found to travel to a nearby town on Sundays. An equally remarkable phenomenon was the interest in Sunday sailings on the Clyde, the steamers being exempt from the constraints of licensing law. In the early twentieth century, temperance movements continued to be enormously influential; not only did the Temperance (Scotland) Act of 1913 allow communities, through the mechanism of a local veto poll, to declare their area "dry", but a temperance candidate, Edwin Scrymgeour, defeated Winston Churchill in the General Election in Dundee in 1922 to become Britain's only Prohobitionist Member of Parliament. A more realistic approach to the "drink problem" than total prohibition was to be found in many of the mining areas of Scotland where, from the late nineteenth century in imitation of a Swedish model, reformed public houses which returned a share of the profits to the community – the Gothenburgs or "Goths" – had emerged.

One of the most enduring folk legends attests to the deep-rootedness of the Scottish interest in drink. The story of heather ale, a semi-mystical product produced by a lost process known to our Pictish ancestors, has attracted writers and re-tellings throughout the years. The sixteenth century historian, Hector Boece, wrote of this wonderful drink:

> The Pichtis maid of this herbe, sum time, ane richt
> delicius and hailsum drink

and told how the Picts would never let anyone, not of their own race, learn the secret of the drink. This legend is turned into a poem by Robert Louis Stevenson, *Heather Ale: A Galloway Legend.* He tells how the last two possessors of the secret, a father and son, were captured by the enemy and threatened with torture unless they surrendered the secret. The father agrees to tell, provided that his son is thrown into the sea to prevent him witnessing the betrayal. This done the last of the Picts turns defiantly to the enemy and says:

> True was the word I told you:
> Only my son I feared;
> For I doubt the sapling courage
> That goes without the beard.

But now in vain is the torture,
Fire shall never avail:
Here dies in my bosom
The secret of Heather Ale

and one may rightly feel that the Scots obsession with drink is nowhere better exemplified than in the father's sacrifice of his and his son's life to preserve the sacred secret of the Heather Ale.

However the Scot's love affair with drink does not always lead to death and ruination, even if that other Dundonian advocate of temperance, William McGonagall, would seek to suggest otherwise:

Oh, thou demon Drink, thou fell destroyer,
Thou curse of society, and its greatest annoyer.
What hast thou done to society, let me think?
I answer thou has caused the most of ills, thou
    demon Drink.

Thou causeth the mother to neglect her child,
Also the father to act as he were wild,
So that he neglects his loving wife and family dear,
By spending his earnings foolishly on whisky, rum,
    and beer.

A more cheerful approach to the joys of drink can be found, unsurprisingly, in Burns:

O, Willie brew'd a peck o' maut,
And Rob and Allan cam to see;
Three blither hearts, that lee-lang night,
Ye wad na find in Christendie.

We are na fou, we're nae that fou,
But just a drappie in our e'e;
The cock may craw, the day may daw,
And aye we'll taste the barley bree.

and if an obsession can be enjoyed in moderation then

so be it. Walter Scott's Bailie Nicol Jarvie in *Rob Roy* was properly opposed to taking strong drink at breakfast time – well almost. It was, he told MacGregor:

> . . .an unlawful and perilous habit to begin the day wi' spirituous liquors, except to defend the stomach (whilk was a tender part) against the norning mist; in whilk case his father the deacon had recommended a dram, by precept and example

which saying he took off his dram. *Slàinte!*

THE LAD
O' PAIRTS

The Scots and Education

The first recorded pedagogue in Scotland was Saint Columba. It is recorded that in the sixth century he imported schooling from Ireland, where "every monastery was a school" and a short while after it could be said that "boys came to Iona for schooling".

The teacher has always commanded a certain respect in this country (some would say fear) and the word didactic isn't such a bad word here as in other places. The theme of this book being obsession, one of the clearest manifestations of obsession is an abundance of archetypes and stereotypes, and with these education is twice blessed, both in the past and in the present education scene; from the village dominie and the lad o' pairts to the the urban jungle and the "Kirriemuir Conspiracy" – a conspiracy which, it is alleged, ensures that the balance of power of influence and power in the educational establishment is always held by the easterly and semi-rural parts of Scotland rather than by the West Central belt. However, there can scarcely be a more deeply rooted conviction about Scots education – even if it is only held *by* Scots – than the one which avers it to be the best or certainly better than most, that it has been better for longer, and that it is accompanied by a love of learning quite out of the usual.

When in 1995 a not so young man in his thirties, calling himself Brandon Lee, opted for a second dose of schooling at his old school, Bearsden Academy, television teams from all over the world were attracted to this douce and leafy suburb. By role playing his second childhood, he gave a whole new meaning to the term "lad o' pairts". Lee, or whatever his real name was, had in a way declared his faith in the Scottish educational system; in another way he was living out J.M. Barrie's fantasy in *Dear Brutus*, when all of the characters are taken to Lob's Wood and offered a "second chance" to fulfil their dreams. Lee's particular, rather masochistic fantasy was to buck the system by taking his Highers again, though the dream had its mundane side, since the goal of this elaborate deception was not, say, to become a poet or a philosopher, but merely a doctor. Anyway, this was a case of a confidence trickster who didn't really cause very much harm to anyone and whose masquerade was intended to bring educational advancement rather than power or financial gain.

One issue which has to be faced is the contention that the Scots view of our educational system is so obsessively self-regarding that it blinds us to its essential second-rate nature, both now and in the past. Indeed Professor Smout, in *A Century of the Scottish People* 1830-1950 has suggested that Scotland's past educational reputation is something of a myth, that claims for its democratic character are overstated and it ought rather to be termed meritocratic. For example, the proportion of early school leavers at one time in the 1950s was so much greater than the proportion who stayed on at school – and more than the equivalent proportion in England – that Smout concludes:

> The system had defined the overwhelming majority of the population as stupid, and reaped the miserable consequence.

Perhaps, but there is no doubt that there is a persistent element of "Wha's like us?" in the Scots character and, while conceding the point about a meritocracy, we might reply that at any rate we had a meritocracy when others were still stuck with an aristocracy. And "others" can as usual be taken to include the English.

The fact is that as far as early and sustained public recognition of the need to educate a people is concerned, Scotland's record is almost unequalled, and superior to our southern neighbour's. As early as 1496, the state, in an attempt to ensure good governance, was making education a part of public policy rather than trust to the barons and freeholders to do it for themselves:

> It is statute and ordanit throw all the realme, that all barronis and frehaldaris, that are of substance put thair eldest sonnis and airis to the sculis, fra thai be aucht or nyne yeiris of age, and till remane at the grammer sculis, quhill thai be competentlie foundit and haue perfite latyne.
>
> 1496 Act of James IV

It has been argued that this is the first instance of a legislation anywhere in Europe seeking to provide for the education of its young people.

For those who were in a position to avail themselves of the opportunity, there were schools, like the High School of Edinburgh, for the children of a wider if still privileged elite – and with enviable standards. In 1531:

> Maister Adam Mrwe, maister of the Hie Scule, oblist him to maik the bairnis perfyte grammariarris [i.e. in Latin] within thre yeiris.

Even before this was written, the existence of an educated and literate group of people can be inferred from the popularity of those fifteenth-century poets known as the Makars. Indeed one of the most illustrious of the Makars, Robert Henryson, was described as a "Schoolmaster in Dunfermline" on the title page of his most regarded book *The Morall Fabillis of Esope the Phrygian*. In a way, too, the tone of these fables, with their admonitions to good behaviour and concluding moral, is quite schoolmasterish, although Henryson's gentle humour marks him out in a profession whose generally stern attitude, even in the twentieth century, was summed up by Alexander Scott as:

"Scots education – I tellt ye! I tellt ye!"

Sir David Lyndsay, author of *The Thrie Estatis*, incidentally offers a commentary on the ineffectiveness of the 1496 Act, when he pictures a "gang" of young noblemen who have more warlike priorities than education in mind:

We think thame very natural foolis
That learnes ower meikle at the scuilis
Schir ye maun learn to rin ane speir
And guide ye like ane man o weir

Perhaps that was a manifestation of another obsession associated with education, namely "skidging", "plunking" or other evocative synonyms for truancy? Sometimes a very extreme form of voluntary "de-schooling" was practised, as when an seventeenth-century Edinburgh bailie was murdered in the course of a riot by a schoolboy "yesternicht efter fyve houres at evin be ane schott of ane pistolett in his foreheid".

Later poets like Fergusson and Burns present further evidence of a widening interest in literature, and proof of an ability to read and comprehend poetry at a time when illiteracy was still rife in England:

I can well remember how that even ploughboys and
maidservants would have gladly bestowed the wages
which they earned the most hardly, and which they

wanted for necessary clothing, if they might but procure
the works of Burns.

Heron's *Memoir of Burns*

How was it that such a general level of literacy was
possible in one of the less wealthy countries of Europe?
Was it connected with the democratic instinct, as
many have claimed, or were there other reasons? A
respondent to the Argyll Commission of 1865, looking
back at various attempts to provide general education,
gave as an opinion that whereas the object of some
measures was:

. . .to effect the education of a class; the object of the
parochial schools was to overtake the education of the
people.

It is a notion which runs like a strong broad stream
through Scottish history since the sixteenth-century.
Elitism perhaps, but in a form which spreads its
influence wide, an ideal of entitlement which sometimes falters or even disappears in time of civil unrest,
which for a long time fails to recognise even the
existence of the Highland people, but which persists,
until by the nineteenth century, literacy for all is
achieved. Primary education was made compulsory in
1872 and finally, in 1894, Henry Craik's reforms at the
Scottish Office enabled elementary education to be
offered free to all aged 5 to 14.

The first formulation of this aspiration appeared in
the 1560 *First Book of Discipline* in which Knox,
Melville and the other reformers planned the "virtuous
education and godly upbringing of the youth of the
realm". A three-layered form of provision was
envisaged, with elementary schools in each parish,
grammar schools in the burghs and a college in each
principal town. Here again the civil unrest of the

Reformation thwarted the reformers' intentions and in 1616 a more pragmatic second attempt was made by the Privy Council:

> In everie parroche of the kingdome. . . a scoole salbe establisheit and a fitt persone appointit to teache the same.

Once more this was far from being entirely successful but the momentum was begun and continued with added energy in the many succeeding attempts. But what of the motives which lay behind these early moves?

Cerainly education for its own sake may have figured in the minds of the legislators, but just as James IV intended to bring about better governance, so too the Privy Councillors had other purposes in mind, such as the abolition of the Gaelic, or:

> . . .Irishe language, whilk is one of the cheif and principall causis of the continewance of barbaritie and incivilitie amongis the inhabitantis of the Ilis and Heylandis.

and, of course, the recurring theme of the promotion of the "trew religioun". And it is in the "trew religioun" that the greatest and indeed obsessive driving force is to be found. The Protestant credo held that a literate populace was a prerequisite of worship – nothing should stand between the individual and the Scriptures. The parish schools were intended to equip the people to read the Bible and to this end the the various "inglis" translations were to be made available, as had been decreed by Act of Parliament as early as 1543:

> . . .baith the new testament and the auld in the vulgar toung in Inglis or Scottis

Not until 1872 was there an Act which truly could be said to have had a secular nature. Some burgh councils

had for some time been building up a greater influence
in running secondary schools, and their particular
brand of parochialism furnished a target for the gently
satiric eye of John Galt:

> In the year 1809 the bigging of the new schoolhouse
> was under consideration. There was about that time
> a great sough throughout the country on the subject
> of education, and it was a fashion to call schools
> academies, and out of a delusion rising from the use
> of that term, to think it necessary to decry the good
> plain old places [i.e. grammar schools]
> *The Provost*

Typically it was the burgh academy which brought
streamlined selection and cultivation of merit to
fruition. Here is Lewis Grassic Gibbon's Chris Guthrie
in *Sunset Song*, who is a "high-flyer" in the making:

> For she'd met with books, she went with them to a
> magic land far from Echt, out and away and south. And
> at school they wrote she was the clever one and John
> Guthrie said she might have the education she needed
> if she stuck to her lessons. . .and at arithmetic she was
> more than good, doing great sums in her head so that
> she was always first in the class, they made her the
> dux and they gave her prizes, four prizes in four
> years she had.

And then came the ultimate accolade. Before she had
just been called the *dux* – now she was actually to be
allowed to study Latin!

> She sat for her bursary, won it, and began the
> conjugating Latin verbs, the easy ones only at first,
> *Amo, amas, I love a lass* and then you laughed out loud
> when the Dominie said that and he cried *Whist, whist*
> but was real pleased and smiled at you and you felt fine
> and tingly and above all the rest of the queans who

weren't learning Latin or anything else, they were
kitchen-maids in the bone.

With just such a final note of condemnation the "God's
Elect" of the Reformation Church were transmuted
into the baser secular metal of "academic excellence",
but not until our own day would anyone dream of a
situation where there would be "excellence for all", as
the Labour Party has recently done! Chris Guthrie
knew only that she was a fortunate member of a group
who had been blessed with brains – she was "clever"
and so was condemned to begin the whole process over
again by herself becoming a teacher:

> Glad she'd be when she'd finished her exams and was
> into Aberdeen University, getting her B.A. and and then
> a school of her own. . .

In a way Professor Smout, the Historiographer Royal, is
right in his questioning of the democratic myth, but
in another way he underestimates the impulse which is
close to obsession, which seeks to widen the educational
experience of as many as possible of Scotland's youth.
For even as the century comes to an end the Scottish
education system is embarking yet again on its
perennial quest to broaden the opportunities for all with
more reforms, this time in the upper secondary school,
in a government programme with the aspirational, if
atrociously punning title, *Higher Still.*

What is more, Scotland may have been among the
last countries in Western Europe to end corporal
punishment in its schools, but typically there are many,
both among the belters and the belted, who continue to
find it an occasion of reminiscence. In a sense corporal
punishment, with use of the belt, strap, tawse or
Lochgelly, began with a broad hint from the aptly titled
First Book of Discipline: "Trial [should] be taken

whether the spirit of docility be found in them or not", and it mercifully ended with scarcely a whimper in the 1980s, but the education went on just the same. In any case, as Chris Guthrie discovered, there is more to life than the school. The Scots character is robust enough to survive any experiences that school can offer and to take the opportunity to absorb a healthy scepticism which will be handy in their declining years. One Erchie MacPherson, Neil Munro's lovely comic creation from the early years of this century, has it about right:

> For mair nor a generation noo, every bairn has had
> to go to the school – a' the parents o' a' the weans in
> school the noo have had an education themselves,
> so that baith at hame and in the school the young
> generation of the present day have sae mony advantages
> ower whit you and I had, they ought to be regular gems
> o' guid behaviour and intelligence. But I canna see that
> they're ony better than their grandfaithers were at the
> same age. Except my guid-dochter's boy, Alick, they're
> a' worse.

However, we cannot close without a word from that other Munro character, Para Handy, who is clear at any rate about the character-building effects of a Scotch education:

> . . .educaation gives you the nerve, and if you have
> the nerve you can go round the world.

THE ENGLISH, FOR ANCE, BY GUILE WAN THE DAY

The Scots and England

There is, as we hope the rest of this book suggests, no shortage of Scotch obsessions but this one is, undoubtedly, the big one. The obsessive relationship between Scotland and England is suggested by the source for our title: Jean Elliot's moving lament for the dead of Flodden *The Flowers of the Forest*.

> Dule and wae for the order sent our lads to the Border;
> The English, for ance, by guile wan the day;
> The Flowers of the Forest, that faucht aye the foremost,
> The prime o' our land, are cauld in the clay.

Flodden was a major Scottish defeat, a battle that had no real purpose other than gesture politics, a battle that was ill-considered and ill-managed, a meaningless Scottish involvement in European grand strategy. A tragedy, undoubtedly, even if a tragedy which has inspired a fine lyric. It is notable that within one stanza the poet has deftly turned the defeat from being Scotland's fault, "Dule and wae for the order. . .", to something for which the blame can enthusiastically be laid at the door of the old enemy.

There are a number of points of interest in this verse – the suggestion that the English "for ance" won, and the suggestion that on this occasion they won by guile.

If one examines the England-Scotland fixture list, then there is, with apologies to Jean Elliot, no doubt that the Lord was on the side of the big battalions – for every Scottish victory, a Bannockburn or a Stirling Bridge, there are twice as many defeats – Falkirk, Pinkie, Neville's Cross, Solway Moss. Flodden was thus no isolated incident in the long history of conflict in this island, nor unusual in that the Scots were on the losing side. The attribution of the English victory to "guile" is, of course, prime Scottish obsessiveness; sound strategy on the part of the English commander, and poor generalship on the part of James IV, has been packaged for domestic consumption as guile. Guile, one might have thought, would be seen as a military virtue. Guile, when it manifests itself as Bruce digging pits to trap the English cavalry at Bannockburn, must be indeed be seen as a military virtue, but outmanoeuvring a Scottish army led by a chivalrous but impatient King is not superior skill but deceitful and underhand "guile".

It can hardly be surprising that the Scots have developed an obsession with England and the English. We have, for example, never troubled to develop an obsession with the Welsh, the Welsh presenting no threat to the nation's life and identity, the Welsh not sharing a hundred mile long border, the Welsh, in short, not being a larger neighbour with hegemonistic ambitions. The Welsh are a foreign race with whom we may or may not claim some, fairly spurious, Celtic kinship and have about as large a part to play in the Scottish psyche as the Portuguese.

The English, on the other hand, are what we are not.

Scottish identity all too often consists in being "not English"; we define ourselves not as a positive, but as a negative. The inbred and carefully acquired aptitude at underdog status which afflicts many Scots owes much to knee-jerk reactions to England and the English – from "for ance, by guile wan the day" to the "we wuss robbed" cry of the terraces. And, talking of terraces, one can find in the behaviour of Scottish football fans abroad a prime example of English-focussed obsession. Scottish football fans have historically had hardly the most savoury of reputations abroad, but in the 1980s when English football supporter thuggery became an international scandal, the Scottish fans became every-body's favourite visitors – high-spirited but peaceful, hard-drinking but (more or less) perfect gentlemen. Was this because of a change in the national character? Was it because of better travel and policing arrange-ments? Well perhaps – but surely the biggest single reason was the collective wish to be seen as different from the English fans; if the English fans were going to be lager louts and yobs then the Scots would be jolly Jocks abroad.

It can hardly be surprising that Scotland defines its identity as "not-England" or that the relationship with England has been difficult and obsessive – the proximity of the larger country and the history of the relationship hardly has been conducive to a relaxed attitude. The apt phrase, coined by the Canadian Prime Minister Pierre Trudeau, that for Canada to share the North American land mass with the United States was like a man having to share a bed with an elephant, has obvious parallels in the island of Britain.

The most convinced Scottish supporter of the Union and the constitutional status quo will become irate at references to "The Queen of England" and when travelling abroad will spend considerable time and effort explaining to French hoteliers and Spanish barmen that they are not English. Faced with hotel registers demanding name, address and nationality they will swither over the choice between Scottish and British. Mild mannered Unionists will become irritated when a UK weather forecast refers to a drought in the

North West and finds that Skye has attracted its usual clouds and the forecaster really meant Lancashire.

Such efforts would not be required if our neighbours in the island could take the trouble to distinguish between England and Britain but in a whole host of ways they are, in general, unable or unwilling to take this intellectual leap. We thus have English football supporters waving the flag of the Union while supporting England, and every international relationship this country enters into is described as Anglo something, as in "Threat to Anglo-American relationship". This marginalisation of the non-English components of the United Kingdom is an insidious form of attack on national identity. Oddly enough the early, post Union, terminology of "North Britain" and "South Britain", however much it might have offended the sensibilities of Scots,was at least even handed in its treatment and accepted the constitutional reality that the former Kingdoms of England and Scotland were merged in a new identity, with a new Parliament and a new set of political structures. However, the popular perception in England was that she, and her Parliamentary institutions had absorbed the northern Kingdom and this view has ever since coloured attitudes and relationships on both sides of the Border.

However the problems between English and Scotch are of longer-standing than the Act of Union. The Scotch obsession with the English finds many excellent literary exemplars – but a fine example is to be found in the *Complaint of Scotland* published in 1549. The anonymous author, a man whom we may perhaps credit with a fair share of obsessiveness, points out:

> . . .there is nocht twa natiouns under the firmament that
> are mair contrar and different fra otheris nor is Inglis
> men and Scottis men, quhoubeit that they be within ane

ile, and nichtbours, and of ane language. For Inglis men are subtil, and Scottish men are facile. Inglis men are ambitious in prosperity, and Scottish men are humain in prosperity. Inglis men are hummil quhen thay are subjeckit be force and violence, and Scottish men furious quhen thay are violently subjeckit. Inglis men are cruel quhen thay get victory, and Scottish men are merciful quhen thay get victory. And to conclude, it is unpossible that Scottish men and Inglis men can remain in concord under ane monarchy or ane prince, because ther naturis and conditiouns are as indefferent as is the nature of scheip and wolvis.

It is, of course, a pre-requisite for the full observance of this obsession that all the good qualities – openness, resolution in adversity, mercy in victory – should rest with one side and all the bad qualities be hung round the neck of the Southron foe.

It is hardly surprising that Scots, enjoying the benefits of all these moral superiorities, should at times have let the iron enter into their souls when the world in general, and the English in particular, have unaccountably failed to recognise their superiority. Doubtless this lack of appreciation lay behind the experience which prompted P. G. Wodehouse to remark:

It is never difficult to distinguish between a Scotsman with a grievance and a ray of sunshine.

The innate sense of moral and intellectual superiority over the English on which the Scots pride themselves is reinforced by comments like that of the historian Philip Guedella:

An Englishman is a man who lives on an island in the North Sea governed by Scotsmen.

– a view given some point by the reflection that of eighteen twentieth-century Prime Ministers no less than six were Scots or of Scots descent. This Scottish take-over of British life also resulted in anecdotes such as the one of the Scot who returned from his first business trip to London.

> "How did you find the English?" asked his curious neighbours.
> "I canna rightly say," replied the traveller. "I only dealt with the heids o' depairtments."

The Scots, a generous people, have always been commendably willing to lend their assistance to the English, aware that much assistance was needed. Para Handy describes an English tourist in the Hebrides, clearly a gentlemen who stood in much need of a guide and counsellor:

> "What wass there on the island at the time but a chenuine English towerist, wi' a capital red kilt, and, man! but he wass green! He wass that green, the coos of Colonsay would go mooin' along the road efter him, thinkin' he wass gress. He wass wan of them English chentlemen that'll be drinkin' chinger-beer on aal occasions, even when they're dry, and him bein' English, he had seen next to nothing aal his days till he took the boat from West Loch Tarbert. The furst night on the island he went oot in his kilt, and came back in half an oor to the inns wi' his legs fair peetiful! There iss nothing that the mudges likes to see among them better than an English towerist with a kilt. . ."
>
> "It's the chinger-beer that's comin' oot on you," says John MacDermott, that had the inns at the time. "There is not a thing you can drink that iss more deliteerious in Colonsay. Nobody takes it here."
>
> "And what in all the world do they take?" said the English chentleman.
>
> "The water o' the mountain well," said John "and whiles a drop of wholesome Brutish spirits. There's some that doesna care for water."

However much the Scot may have contributed to the British picture or however much they may have assisted their Southern neighbours there always remains a problem of identity, coupled with a regret for that which has gone. James Boswell typifies this two-sided approach to an obsession with England and the English. When he arranged his famous meeting with Samuel Johnson in Thomas Davies' bookshop in Covent Garden his first words were:

> Mr Johnson, I do indeed come from Scotland,
> but I cannot help it.

which rather unfortunately left the way open for the Johnsonian riposte:

> That, Sir, I find, is what a very great many of
> your countrymen cannot help.

There can be few Scots who have so anxiously sought assimilation into England – Boswell's first life plan was to join the Brigade of Guards, later he wished to practice at the English Bar and toyed with English politics. He noted in his diary for 25th June 1774:

> It is true Hume, Robertson, and other greater geniuses
> than I am prefer Scotland. But they have neither that
> peculiar and permanent love of London and all its
> circumstances which I have; nor are they so much in
> unison with the English as I am, which I have clearly
> perceived, and of which Mr Johnson has assured me.

However – and with Boswell there is always a "however" – his views were, even on the great object of being integrated into England, mixed. In March 1772 he confided to his diary:

> Mr Urquhart spoke to me strongly to come to the
> English bar. I argued against it. But was pleased to hear
> him, because I really do often wish to do it.

Confused? It gets worse:

> Mr Johnson is not against it; and says my having any
> Scotch accent would be but for a little while. My only
> objection is that I have a kind of idea of Scottish
> patriotism that makes me think it a duty to spend my
> money in my own country. Auchinleck indeed is my
> great object; and I have a notion I might be as much
> there if I were at the English bar as I can be while I
> practise in the Court of Session.

Boswell, perhaps more than any other literary Scot,
sums up the inconsistencies of the Scotch obsession
with England and the English. He longs to move to
London, while fantasising about buying St Kilda; he
deeply desires to be taken for English in his speech and
manners, but when writing to set up a meeting with
Rousseau he opens his letter to the philosopher with the
proud claim:

> I am a Scots gentleman of ancient family.

When in Leipzig on his Grand Tour he reads to his
companions an extract from the Declaration of
Arbroath and later records in his diary:

> They were struck with the noble sentiments of liberty
> of the old Scots, and they expressed their regret at the
> shameful Union. I felt true patriot sorrow. O infamous
> rascals, who sold the honour of your country to a nation
> against which our ancestors supported themselves with
> so much glory! But I say no more, only Alas!, poor
> Scotland.

Boswell's sentiments echo those of his younger fellow-
Ayrshiremen, Robert Burns, whom, oddly enough, he
never seems to have chanced to meet.

> Fareweel to a' our Scottish fame,
> Fareweel our ancient glory;

Fareweel even to the Scottish name,
Sae fam'd in martial story!

What force or guile could not subdue,
Thro' many warlike ages,
Is wrought now by a coward few,
For hireling traitors wages.
The English steel we could disdain,
Secure in valour's station;
But English gold has been our bane,
Such a parcel of rogues in a nation!

However it can hardly surprise the reader to turn to a poem published just a few years later to read Burns's stern injunction:

Be Britain still to Britain true,
Amang oursels united;
For never but by British hands,
Shall British wrongs be righted.

The Scots Parliament, in its Act for a Treaty with England in 1705, envisaged a Union as:

. . .the most effectual way for extinguishing the heats and differences that are unhappily raised betwixt the two nations . . .

However, the Union probably raised as many problems as it solved, not least the identity crisis which surely lies close to the heart of the Scotch obsession with the English. "Heats and differences" continued, post-Union Scots had to work out what position they were going to adopt, what nation they belonged to. As we have seen with Boswell, at times this resulted in quite convoluted mental wrestlings.

Other Scots seemed to cope with the situation better, and quite comfortably became an incorporated part of British, English, London life – but there was always likely to be a sticking point, an issue which suddenly, and perhaps unpredictably, awoke an atavistic response. Tobias Smollett, the son of a Dumbartonshire laird, trained in medicine at Glasgow, moved to London, joined the Royal Navy as a surgeon's mate, and by the time of the 1745 Jacobite Rising was back in London, comfortably established in medical practice in Downing Street. By religion, background, service history and environment, Smollett might have been expected to be sympatheitic to the Hanoverian establishment. His friend the Rev. Alexander Carlyle described him thus:

> Smollett, though a Tory, was not a Jacobite, but he
> had the feelings of a Scotch gentleman. . .

Smollett was, however, so moved by the news of the slaughter at Culloden, and by the vulgar chauvinism of the London mob, that he burst out with his first published work, *The Tears of Scotland*

> Mourn, hapless Caledonia, mourn
> Thy banished peace, thy laurels torn!
> Thy sons, for valour long renown'd,
> Lie slaughter'd on their native ground;
> Thy hospitable roofs no more
> Invite the stranger to the door;
> In smoky ruins sunk they lie,
> The monuments of cruelty.

Subsequent verses include images such as "Thy ravish'd virgins shriek in pain" and

> Yet, when the rage of battle ceas'd
> The victor's soul was not appeas'd;
> The naked and forlorn must feel
> Devouring flames, and murd'ring steel!

When friends suggested to Smollett that this was rather strong meat and likely to give offence, and indeed endanger him, Smollett's response was to go off and add a seventh and final verse, as it were, to "mak' siccar":

> While the warm blood bedews my veins,
> And unimpair'd remembrance reigns,
> Resentment of my country's fate
> Within my filial breast shall beat;
> And, spite of her insulting foe,
> My sympathizing verse shall flow:
> "Mourn, hapless Caledonia, mourn
> Thy banish'd peace, thy laurels torn."

Smollett, we may conclude, however well established he was in England, still continued to feel and respond as a Scot and to cherish the differences between the two nations.

Sir Walter Scott, loyal subject of the Royal George's, Tory and Judge, equally shared the common Scottish faith that the distinctiveness of Scotland had, at all costs, to be maintained. Most obviously this belief was worked out in a sequence of novels on Scottish themes, *Waverley, Rob Roy, The Heart of Midlothian, Old Mortality, Redgauntlet*, etc. Scott's dichotomy was expressed in his characters, as for example in this exchange in *Rob Roy* between Bailie Nicol Jarvie and Andrew Fairservice:

> There's naething sae gude on this side o' time but it
> might hae been better, and that may be said o' the Union.
> Nane were keener against it than the Glasgow folk. . .
> Now, since St Mungo catched herrings in the Clyde,
> what was ever like to gar us flourish like the sugar and
> tobacco-trade. Will ony body tell me that, and grumble
> at the treaty that opened us a road west-awa' yonder?

So observed the merchant Bailie. Andrew Fairservice responded with a truly Scottish combination of nostalgia and anti-English feeling:

That it was an unco change to hae Scotland's laws made
in England; and that, for his share, he wadna for a' the
herring-barrels in Glasgow, and a' the tobacco-casks to
boot, hae gienn up the riding o' the Scots Parliament,
or sent awa' our crown, and our sword, and our
sceptre, and Mons Meg, to be keepit by thae English
pock-puddings in the Tower o' Lunnon. What wad Sir
William Wallace, or auld Davie Lindsay, hae said to the
Union, or them that made it.

In one of Scott's plunges into contemporary politics,
over the question of bank regulation, he observed in his
Letters of Malachi Malagrowther:

. . .the conduct of England toward Scotland as a
kingdom, whose crown was first united to theirs by our
giving them a King, and whose dearest national rights
were surrendered to them by an incorporating Union,
has not been of late such as we were entitled to expect.

There has arisen gradually, on the part of England,
a desire of engrossing the exclusive management of
Scottish affairs. . . many of which intimate a purpose
to abate us, like old Lear, of our train, and to accustom
us to submit to petty slights and mortifications . . .

However politically committed to the Union and to its
institutions Scott might have been there still ran deep
within his nature a sympathetic and imaginative
response to the old order and a passionate concern that
all national characteristics and distinctions should not
become blurred in some homogenised pan-English
state. Elsewhere in these letters he bursts out :

For God's sake, sir, let us remain as Nature made us,
Englishmen, Irishmen and Scotchmen, with something
like the impress of our several countries upon each!

This surely must be a very common Scottish sentiment
– even in periods when the word "Englishman" had

more international prestige than it perhaps has today. The eighteenth-century Scottish philosopher David Hume was counselled by a well-meaning Scottish friend, Gilbert Elliott, to come home from France and "continue still an Englishman". This produced the following broadside from Hume:

> From what human Motive or Consideration can I prefer living in England to that in foreign Countries?. . . I do not believe there is one Englishman in fifty, who, if he heard that I had broke my Neck tonight, would not be rejoic'd with it. Some hate me because I am not a Tory, some because I a not a Whig, some because I am not a Christian, and all because I am a Scotsman. Can you seriously talk of my continuing an Englishman? Am I, or are you, an Englishman? Will they allow us to be so? Do they not treat with Derision our Pretensions to that Name, and with Hatred our just Pretensions to surpass and to govern them.

Gilbert Elliott, who was so flayed by Hume's invective, was not the only Scot to feel that the title of "Englishman" was worth laying claim to. Robert Louis Stevenson, living and writing in the second half of the nineteenth century, seemingly quite naturally describes himself as "English" when on his *Inland Voyage* or his *Travels with a Donkey in the Cevennes* – but was at the same time very clear in his own mind as to the distinction between Scot and English. He has even sought, in *Weir of Hermiston,* to attempt to find a reason for the distinctiveness of the Scot. Discussing, in the context of a type of clan spirit, the Weirs' aged retainer Kirstie Elliott, and her loyalty to the house of Hermiston, Stevenson observes:

> For that is the mark of the Scot of all classes: that he stands in an attitude towards the past unthinkable to Englishmen, and remembers and cherishes the memory

of his forebears, good or bad; and there burns alive
in him a sense of identity with the dead even to the
twentieth generation.

Surely not only in the context of family history does this
Scottish attitude of mind distinguish the Scot from the
English and colour the way in which the Scot thinks
of the English. Perhaps because of an uncertainty
about what they are, the Scots are obsessed with what
they were. To illustrate with a broad generalisation –
most Scots would know the dates of the battles of
Bannockburn (1314) and Flodden (1513); many might
even know Stirling Bridge (1297) or, at a push, Largs
(1263). It is in the highest degree unlikely that similar
proportions of the English population could go much
beyond Hastings (1066). A request for the date of the
battle of Crecy or Poitiers would be met with a very
dubious response. The difference surely lies in the fact
that battles with the English are an integral part of the
Scottish identity and self-image, whereas the dynastic
manoeuvrings of the Hundred Years War form no very
significant part of the English self-image.

However this strong historical component to the
Scottish psyche is no new thing, no outcome alone of
a desperate post-Union search for identity. The
Declaration of Arbroath is couched in terms of the
historical roots and descent of the Scottish people, their
long independence:

> Within this our realm there have reigned one hundred
> and thirteen Kings of our native royal dynasty, and not
> one of alien birth.

Lord Belhaven, arguing in the Scots Parliament in 1707
against the passing of the Act of Union, did so with
historical imagery and historical parallels:

> I think I see a Free and Independent Kingdom delivering

up That, which all the World hath been fighting for, since the days of Nimrod; yea, that for which most of all the Empires, Kingdoms, States, Principalities and Dukedoms of Europe, are at this very time engaged in the most Bloody and Cruel Wars that ever were, to wit, A Power to Manage their own Affairs by themselves, without the Assistance and Counsel of any other.

But above all, My Lord, I think I see our Ancient Mother CALEDONIA, like Caesar sitting in the midst of our Senate, Ruefully looking round about her, Covering her self with her Royal Garment, attending the Fatal Blow, and breathing out her last with a *Et to quoque mi fili.*

The Scot, obsessed with not being mistaken for an Englishman, obsessively proud of his nation and his race's achievements, unsure exactly what he is, but sure of what he is not would seem predestined to be an unwelcome neighbour to the normally tolerant English. The remarkable patience of the English is of course largely a function of their innate sense of superiority, a superiority well expressed by Cecil Rhodes:

Remember that you are an Englishman, and have consequently won first prize in the lottery of life.

With this degree of conviction, the febrile claims of the Scots can be safely ignored or, better still, tolerantly indulged – it is indeed remarkable that few Englishmen have been quite so dismissive as Anthony Powell in his mock-Augustan diatribe *Caledonia*:

And yet the abject *Picktish* Tribes complain
That ENGLAND'S loss has not proved *Scotland's* gain,
And with each *alcoholick* Breath he draws,
Some Scotchman advocate's Disunion's Cause,
Till *Whisky's* Fumes alone seem to proclaim
The *Pinchbeck* Ornaments of *Scotland's* name.

Whatever the growing internationalisation of culture (and the Americanisation of Scotland is dealt with elsewhere in *Scotch Obsessions*), there seems little doubt that most Scots would still wish to define and describe themselves, in as generous and un-chauvinistic a fashion as possible, as different from the English. Not (necessarily) better, not worse, just distinct. A formulation of the character of the nation as given by John Buchan would appeal to many:

> Look at the long wars of independence which we fought under Bruce and Wallace. If we had any common sense we would have made peace at the beginning, accepted the English terms, and grown prosperous at the expense of our rich neighbours. Look at the wars of religion, when for a refinement of dogma and a nice point of Church government the best of the Lowland peasantry took to the hills. Look at the Jacobite risings. What earthly sense was in them? Merely because Prince Charlie was a Stewart, and because he was young and gallant, we find sober, middle-aged men, lairds, lawyers and merchants, risking their necks and their fortunes to help a cause which was doomed from the start. We have, all of us, we Scots, a queer *daftness* in our blood. We may be trusted to be prudent and sensible beyond the average up to a certain point. But there comes a moment when some half-forgotten loyalty is awakened, and then we fling prudence to the winds.

Or not. The experience of the 1979 referendum on devolution would suggest that prudence, an adherence to the status quo, and a preference for what one disappointed SNP activist called "ninety minute patriotism" may be just as characteristic obsessions.

TEUCHTER AND SASSENACH

The Highland and the Lowland Scot

> . . .for the highland pipale is all very clannish to one
> another and if their chiefs had no intrest in it they
> wold to a sertentlay rather walk 40 miles than pay
> one shilling. . .

So, in 1820, wrote (in characteristically bad spelling)
Henry Bell, steamship pioneer (and Lowlander) to J. A.
Stewart MacKenzie of Seaforth, owner of large Highland
estates (and, despite his name, as much a Lowlander as
Bell). Bell also observed in the same letter that:

> . . .the most part of the land gentlemen is so much
> taken up with politicks, gamblin and other trifling
> amusements that they both neglect their own Intrest
> and the Intrest of their countray. . .

Bell was proposing to Seaforth the economic, social and
practical advantages of the introduction of a steamer
service to the Western Highlands and Islands. His criticism
of the Highlanders sums up much of the typical
Lowland attitude to the Highlands – the clannishness of
the people, their subservience to the chief, their feckless
idleness, their resistance to new ideas, their political
preoccupations and unreliability. Bell was not the first,
nor would he be the last, promoter of big ideas for the
Highlands who found the Highlanders were not entirely

responsive to his plans. The experience of Lord Leverhulme and his purchase of Lewis and Harris after the First World War with the intention of developing fishing and fish processing and reforming crofting is an excellent example of the conflict between Sassanach and Teuchter. Leverhulme's ambitious plans broke down over the resistance of the islanders to surrender their independence for a weekly wage packet. However, one might feel that his renaming the village of Obbe "Leverburgh" betrays a certain high-handed egoism which did not augur well for the success of the project.

Bell and Leverhulme represent the many southerners – Saxons, – Sassenachs – who have turned their minds to the Highland question. Lowland Scots (of course Leverhulme was English not Scottish, – but from the perspective of Harris the difference is perhaps less obvious or significant) have undoubtedly always had an obsession about the Highlands, although there is inter-estingly much less evidence of a reciprocal obsession. The Lowland obsession was generally based on very little real knowledge of the Highlands or the Highlander – the stereotypical dismissal as of them as "Donald", "Sawney" or "Teuchters" is evidence enough of this. Samuel Johnson, who was in principle no fonder of Highland Scots than Lowland Scots and may thus be taken as a neutral observer, remarked, on his Highland tour in 1773:

> To the southern inhabitants of Scotland, the state of the mountains and the islands is equally unknown with that of *Borneo* or *Sumatra*; Of both they have only heard a little, and guess the rest. They are strangers to the language and the manners, to the advantages and the wants of the people, whose life they would model, and whose evils they would remedy.

Johnson was writing in the aftermath of the post-

Culloden remodelling of the life of the Highlands, but the habit of the Lowlander trying to change the ways of the Highlander was certainly not invented in 1746.

> It is inactit that everie gentilman or yeaman within the said Islandis, or ony of thame, haveing childreine maill or famell, and being in goodis worth thriescore ky, sall put at the leist thair eldest sone, or haveing no children maill thair eldest dochter, to the scuillis on the Lawland, and interteny and bring thame up thair quhill that may be found able sufficientlie to speik, reid and wryte Inglisch. . .

So, in 1609, ran one of the *Statutes of Iona*, one of James VI's attempts to civilise the Highlander. Seven years later the Scottish parliament enacted an Education Act ordaining the creation of parish schools throughout Scotland and which in part ran:

> . . .that the vulgar Inglishe toung be universallie plantit, and the Irisch language. . . may be abolisheit and removit. . .

The barbarous and uncivilised nature of the Highlander had long been remarked upon – by the Lowlander. The fourteenth-century chronicler, John of Fordoun, described the two peoples co-existing in Scotland. He distinguished between the inhabitants of the lowland coastal area:

> . . .domesticated and cultured, trustworthy, patient and urbane, decent in their attire, law-abiding and peaceful, devout in religious observance. . .

and the Highlanders who were a:

> . . .wild and untamed people, rough and unbending, given to robbery, ease-loving, of artful and impressionable temperament, comely in form but unsightly in dress.

Fordoun, just in case there was any doubt, is in the extremely lowland agricultural area of the Howe of the Mearns, in Kincardineshire, but close enough to the Highland glens of Angus and the Grampians for the douce farmers to be frightened of Highland raiders.

All along the edge of the Highlands – where Lowlander and Highlander met – there was a long history of conflict and suspicion. In the Lennox, the full moon was known as "MacFarlane's Lantern", in grudging tribute to that clan's ability to use the moonlit nights to steal cattle from the lowland farms. Protection rackets were operated by the MacGregors and others – a leading man of the clan would guarantee to protect lowland farmers from cattle-stealing raids, provided enough money was paid. For a typically Lowland reaction to this one can do no better than turn to a Glaswegian observer, Bailie Nicol Jarvie in Walter Scott's *Rob Roy*:

> . . .mony hundreds o' them come down to the borders
> of the low country, where there's gear to grip, and live by
> stealing, reiving, lifting cows, and the like depredations!
> A thing deplorable in any Christian country – the mair
> especially, that they take pride in it, and reckon driving
> a spreagh (whilk is, in plain Scotch, stealing a herd of
> nowte) a gallant, manly action, and mair befitting of
> pretty men (as sic reivers will ca' themsells) than to
> win a day's wage by ony honest thrift.

Even in the normally calm waters of poetry the Highland/Lowland divide manifests itself. A sixteenth-century poem crudely demonstrates the racial stereotypes:

> God and Sanct Petir was gangand be the way
> Heiche up in Ardgyle quhair thair gait lay.
> Sanct Petir said to God in a sport word
> "Can ye not make a heilanman of this horss turd?"
> God turnd owre the horss turd with his pykit staff,

And up start the helandman blak as ony draff.
Quod God to the helandman "Quair wilt thow now?"
"I will doun in the lawland, Lord, and thair steill a kow."

A century earlier, William Dunbar's poem *The Flyting of Dunbar and Kennedy* has much to say about Kennedy the "Iersch brybour baird" – or Irish/Erse (i.e.Gaelic) beggar bard – and includes a fairly good pun on the word Erse (frequently used as a synonym for Gaelic):

Thy trechour tung hes tane ane heland strynd
(Thy traitor tongue has taken a highland strain)
Ane lawland ers would mak a bettir noyis
(A lowland arse would make a better noise)

The unfortunate Walter Kennedy, excoriated in this poem, was the third son of Lord Kennedy of Dunure in Ayrshire – an indication of the extent of Gaelic in fifteenth century Scotland. Dunbar's contempt for the Gaelic speaking poet is, happily, moderated in his reference to Kennedy in his *Lament for the Makaris*:

Gud Maister Walter Kennedy
In poynt of dede lyis veraly,
Great reuth it wer that so suld be;
Timor mortis conturbat me.

Dunbar's contempt for Gaelic was not unique. Suspicion and ignorance go hand in hand and the general lack of knowledge of the Highlands and Highlanders in Lowland Scotland, coupled with a not unreasonable suspicion that the Highlander would prefer to go his own way and was not entirely politically reliable, made the control of the Highlands a major issue for many Scottish kings. Of course, the Lowland nobles were equally politically unreliable, but they were at least more familiar and predictable.

Southern suspicion of the Highlander was fuelled by the actions of the semi-independent Lords of the Isles.

This succession of Macdonald rulers, whose territories embraced much of the Hebrides and the Western Highlands, had only the most nominal loyalty to the Scottish kings and were quite happy to conduct an independent foreign policy, negotiating with English kings. In the Treaty of Westminster/Ardtornish in 1462, John, 4th Lord of the Isles, agreed with Edward IV of England that if Edward conquered Scotland then the Lord of the Isles and the Earl of Douglas would divide Scotland beyond the Forth between them and hold it as vassals of the English crown. Scotland had much experience of over-mighty subjects, but the Highland version was particularly troublesome because of the geographical difficulties of doing anything to control them in their remote and sea-girt fastnesses.

James IV was to spend a good part of his reign on expeditions into the Highlands trying to bring Fordoun's "wild and untamed people" under control. How much success he had may be judged from his great-grandson, James VI, who wrote in his manual of kingship the *Basilicon Doron*:

> As for the Highlands, I shortly comprehend them all
> in two sorts of people: the one, that dwelleth in our
> mainland, that are barbarous for the most part, and
> yet mixed with some show of civility: the other, that
> dwelleth in the Isles, and are utterly barbarians,
> without any sort or show of civility.

One of James's answers to the problems of the "barbarians" of the Isles was move settlers there:

> . . .planting colonies among them of answerable inland
> subjects, that within short time may reform and civilise
> the best inclined among them. . .

and he put this plan to work with the leasing of Lewis to "The Gentlemen Adventurers of Fife" and by the planting of a burgh at Stornoway. The "Gentlemen Adventurers", unsurprisingly, met with considerable local resistance and the grand scheme was abandoned.

The mutual suspicion of Lowlander and Highlander was, at times, of value to the state. In the religious conflicts of the 1670s Highland troops were moved into the Covenanting areas of Renfrewshire and Ayrshire to overawe the local population, the alien nature of this so-called "Highland Host" being felt to be particularly effective in achieving control.

Highland/Lowland conflict of course found its high-water mark in the Jacobite risings. While it is, of course, true that these movements were more complex than a straightforward division along a simplistic Highland/Lowland fault-line, with pro-Hanoverian clans and pro-Jacobite Lowlanders, it does remain true that in fact as well as in perception, the strength of Jacobite support lay in the Highlands.

The correspondence of the Secretary of State for Scotland, the Master of Stair, in the period leading up to the events now known as the Massacre of Glencoe, demonstrate an undoubtedly obsessive anxiety to make an example of the Glencoe MacDonalds. First, writing to Lt. Col. Hamilton at Fort William:

> . . .The MacDonalds will fall in this net. That's the only popish clan in the kingdom, and it will be popular to take severe course with them. Let me hear from you. . . whether you think that this is the proper season to maul them in the cold long nights. . .

and then to the Commander in Chief in the Highlands:

> . . .my Lord Argile tells me that Glenco hath not taken the oathes, at which I rejoice, it's a great work of charity to be exact in rooting out that damnable sect, the worst in all the Highlands. . .

Stair's attitude was to be echoed after Culloden by a seriously frightened Government and the genocide instigated by the Duke of Cumberland was, to a significant degree, implemented by Lowland Scots such as Major Lockhart and Captain Caroline Scott on land, and Captain Fergusson at sea.

A disarmed Highlands and a broken clan system might be thought to have presented little future threat to the Lowlands, but still the Highland question continued to exercise minds. The Clearances and the coming of Lowland flockmasters and the black-faced sheep into the Highlands to replace the indigenous population is a familiar and tragic story. The attempts, somewhat reminiscent of James VI's plans, to establish fishing ports through the agency of the British Fisheries Society (founded in 1786) is a more positive, if less well-known, example of a continuing southern preoccupation with the Highlands.

Within thirty or forty years of Culloden there can be observed a significant change in Lowland attitudes to the Highlands. Still the Lowlanders were obsessed with the Highlands, still, as we saw from Henry Bell, they were critical, but now there were new elements. We have dealt elsewhere with the recruitment of Highlanders into the British Army, but there is no doubt that the success of this policy coloured attitudes to the Highlander. In 1762 the young James Boswell was in London and attended Covent Garden Theatre. His diary records:

> Just before the overture began to be played, two
> Highland officers came in. The mob in the upper
> gallery roared out, "No Scots! No Scots! Out with
> them!," hissed and pelted them with apples. My heart
> warmed to my countrymen, my Scotch blood boiled
> with indignation. I jumped up on the benches, roared

out, "Damn you, you rascals!," hissed and was in the
greatest of rage. I am very sure at that time I should
have been the most distinguished of heroes. I hated
the English; I wished from my soul that the Union
was broke and that we might give them another battle
of Bannockburn.

The Highlander (perhaps because he no longer
presented a threat) was coming to be seen as the
emblematic Scot. The interest in the Highlands was
enormously stimulated by the success of the Ossianic
poems collected (or invented) by James Macpherson
and published in the 1760s. English sceptics, like
Charles Churchill, might scoff and declare *Fingal* and
Temora fakes:

> Ossian, sublimest, simplest bard of all
> Whom English infidels, Macpherson call

but Macpherson's tales of Highland heroes and warriors
took all Europe by storm. The Highlands were being
subtly transformed from a primitive and dangerous
wilderness inhabited by uncouth barbarians to a
primitive and romantic wilderness inhabited by
Rousseau-like noble savages. Travellers, like Pennant
and Boswell and Johnson, came to see the Highlands in
the 1760s and 1770s and to record their impressions.
The trickle of travellers became a flood in the early years
of the next century.

A sentimental Jacobitism replaced the real thing and
Burns could safely sing of the lament of *The lovely lass
o' Inverness*:

> Drumossie moor, Drumossie day,
> A waefu' day it was to me;
> For there I lost my father dear,
> My father dear and brethern three!

or in a more jaunty mood:

> Come weal, come woe, we'll gather and go,
> And live or die wi' Charlie

The transformation in the southern view of the Highlands was completed by Walter Scott and Royalty. Scott, first with his poem *The Lady of the Lake* and then with *Waverley* and *Rob Roy*, developed the literary interest in the Highlands first stimulated by the Ossianic poems. Admittedly Scott's Highlands were the accessible Highlands, the Trossachs, but he managed to turn Rob Roy MacGregor from a cattle-thief and bandit into a heroic figure of romance. The Royal Family's love affair with the Highlands, begun with George IV's visit to Scotland in 1822 and consumated by Queen Victoria's purchase of Balmoral, completed the transformation. Writing in her Journal in 1873 of a visit to the scenes of Charles Edward Stuart's post-Culloden wanderings, the Queen recorded:

> I feel a sort of reverence in going over these scenes in this most beautiful country, which I am proud to call my own, where there was such devoted loyalty to the family of my ancestors. . . for Stuart blood is in my veins, and I am now their representative. . .

Tartan (even those just invented for the purpose) and the kilt became symbols of all Scotland – a truly remarkable transformation. The dress which, for most of the population of Scotland, had been the symbol of a threatening alien sub-culture, the dress which had been legally proscribed between 1746 and 1782, became fashionable, respectable and patriotic. The Sassenach's obsession with the Teuchter had turned full circle.

But what of the Highlanders? What of their presumably reciprocal obsession with the Sassenach? The answer is that the Highlander seems to have thought little and cared less about the Lowlander – to have been imbued with a conviction of his own natural superiority and to have wished for little from the Lowlands – other, perhaps, than to be left alone. The ever-observant Samuel Johnson observed:

> By their Lowland neighbours they would not willingly be taught; for they have long considered them as a mean and degenerate race. These prejudices are wearing fast away; but so much of them still remains, that when I asked a very learned minister in the islands, which they considered as their most savage clans: "*Those*, said he, *that live next the Lowlands.*"

The Lowlands formed a market for Highland cattle, a place of employment for Highland labour – in the early nineteenth century there was a substantial and regular seasonal migration of agricultural workers from the Highlands to work on Lowland farms. In 1827 the *Inverness Courier* reported that in two August weeks:

> . . .upwards of 2,500 Highland shearers passed through the Crinan Canal for the south, in the steamboats *Ben Nevis, Comet* and *Highlander*, from the islands of Mull, Skye, etc.

In a similar way, in later years, Highland women followed the fishing fleets around the British Isles gutting and salting. But all these dealings with the Lowlands were based on a cash relationship and implied no acceptance or adoption of inferior southern standards.

The innate sense of superiority, or perhaps self-preoccupation, of the Highlander has meant that they, frustrating as it must be to the Lowland Scot, demon-strate very little obsession with the Lowlands or the Lowlander. Suspicion, yes, but obsessive interest, no. A typical statement of the natural superiority of the Highlands and Highlanders comes from Neil Munro's Highland puffer skipper, Peter Macfarlane, Para Handy. The captain has been discussing music:

. . .good pipers iss difficult nooadays to get; there's not many in it. You'll maybe can get a kind of a plain piper going aboot the streets of Gleska noo and then, but they're like the herrin', and the turnips and rhubarb, and things like that – you don't get them fresh in Gleska; if you want them at their best, you have to go up to the right Hielands and pull them off the tree.

BREATHES THERE THE MAN?

The Scots and their Land

A natural affection for the place of one's birth would seem to be a commonplace enough emotion – most nations could, with appropriate translation, sing with Kipling:

> Land of our birth, we pledge to thee
> Our love and toil in the years to be

and one assumes that Belgians have a particular emotional attachment to the Ardennes and Mongolians to the steppes and hills around Ulan Bator.

The Scots, however, seem to have developed a particularly besotted relationship with their land. The beauties of Scotland are held to be of a self-evidently superior excellence, to enjoy a unique quality and to quite outstrip all rivals. The Scot inherently believes that the Scottish landscape far outshines such pale, southern imitations as Snowdonia, the Lake District and the Yorkshire Dales – as of course it unquestionably does. This categorical assertion of superiority even afflicted as seemingly cosmopolitan a figure as Lord Byron. But it must be remembered that Byron accurately categorised himself as:

> . . .half a Scot by birth, and bred
> a whole one. . .

and it was Byron who, in his poem to Lochnagar, *Lachin Y Gair*, wrote what is perhaps the definitive statement of Scottish topographical triumphalism:

> Years have roll'd on, Loch na Garr, since I left you,
> Years must elapse ere I tread you again:
> Nature of verdure and flowers has bereft you,
> Yet still are you dearer than Albion's plain.
> England! thy beauties are tame and domestic
> To one who has roved o'er the mountains afar:
> Oh! for the crags that are wild and majestic!
> The steep frowning glories of dark Loch na Garr.

Byron was, of course, following in the grand tradition. His slightly older contemporary, Walter Scott, was no mean hand at this assertiveness:

> Breathes there the man with soul so dead,
> Who never to himself hath said,
> This is my own, my native land!
> Whose heart hath ne'er within him burn'd,
> As home his footsteps he hath turn'd
> From wandering on a foreign strand!

was his question in *The Lay of the Last Minstrel*, wherein he goes on to boast:

> O Caledonia! stern and wild
> Meet nurse for a poetic child!
> Land of brown heath and shaggy wood,
> Land of the mountain and the flood,

which could arguably be dismissed as the sort of thing that Mongolian poets write of Mongolia were one not convinced that Scott truly believed in the innate superiority of the land of Scotland. After all it was Scott who said:

> If I did not see the heather, at least once a year, I think
> I should die!

Scott, of course, practically invented the tourist trade and his depiction of the scenic glories of Scotland attracted travellers from all over Europe. A few had found Scotland earlier, and some of them, like the French geologist Barthelemy Faujas de Saint-Fond, took to the land with a positively Scots-like enthusiasm. Of Loch Lomond Saint-Fond wrote:

> Even among the oranges, the myrtles, and the jasmines
> of Italy, I shall often meditate on the wild and romantic
> beauties of this spot.

Even native Scots who passionately long for, and actively seek, the "oranges, the myrtles, and the jasmines of Italy" still feel the pull of the "hills of home", none more so than that inveterate exile and traveller, Robert Louis Stevenson. Writing of Scotland from the perspective of California in *Silverado Squatters* he remarks, in a chapter entitled "The Scot Abroad":

> . . .the old land is still the true love, the others are
> but pleasant infidelities

and goes on to look at the nature of the Scot's love for his native place.

> There is no special loveliness in that grey country,
> with its rainy, sea-beat archipelago; its fields of dark
> mountains; its unsightly places, black with coal; its
> quaint, grey, castled city, where the bells clash of a
> Sunday, and the wind squalls, and the salt showers
> fly and beat.

which seems more than somewhat dismissive. However what Stevenson calls this "mystery of the human heart" – the Scot's love for Scotland – is all powerful:

> . . .it seems at once as if no beauty under the kind
> heavens, and no society of the wise and good, can repay
> me for my absence from my country. . . in my heart of

hearts I long to be buried among good Scots clods. I
will say it fairly, it grows on me with every year: there
are no stars so lovely as Edinburgh street-lamps.

Stevenson, of course, no matter where he travelled, was
quite hopelessly fixated on that "grey country" and its
"fields of dark mountains". In a letter, to J.M. Barrie,
written just two years before his death, he confessed:

It is a singular thing that I should live here in the South
Seas under conditions so new and so striking, and yet
my imagination so continually inhabit that cold grey
huddle of grey hills from which we come. . .

Cold and grey Scotland might have been, but it
produced in Stevenson a yearning which inspired some
of his finest writing, as in these lines addressed to the
Scottish novelist S.R. Crockett:

Blows the wind to-day, and the sun and the rain are
    flying,
Blows the wind on the moor to-day and now,
Where about the graves of the martyrs the whaups are
    crying,
My heart remembers how!

Grey recumbent tombs of the dead in desert places.
Standing stones on the vacant wine-red moor,
Hills of sheep, and the homes of the silent vanished
    races,
And winds, austere and pure

Be it granted to me to behold you again in dying,
Hills of home! and to hear again the call;
Hear about the graves of the martyrs the peewees crying,
And hear no more at all.

There is much literary warrant for the idea of a special
Scottish relationship between the ordinary Scotsman
and the land: Neil Munro in *John Splendid* puts into the

mouth of his hero, Colin, the following meditation on
the land and its impact on "coarse men":

> I know corries in Argile that whsiper silken to the winds
> with juicy grasses, corries where the deer love to prance
> deep in the cool dew, and the beasts of far-off woods
> come in bands at their seasons and together rejoice. I
> have seen the hunter in them and the shepherd too,
> coarse men in life and occupation, come sudden among
> the blowing rush and whispering reed, among the bog-
> flower and the cannoch, unheeding the moor-hen and
> the cailzie-cock rising, or the stag of ten at pause, while
> they stood, passionate adventurers in a rapture of the
> mind, held as it were by the spirit of such places. . .

A contemporary, and admirer of Munro, albeit a writer of
markedly different style and manner, R.B. Cunningham
Graham, movingly records in his short story *Beattock for
Moffat* the call of home to a consumptive exile who is
travelling north from London by rail to end his days in
his native place. As they cross Shap Summit, the dying
man tells his brother Jock:

> The Shap, ye ken, I aye looked at as the beginning of
> the run home. The hills, ye ken, are sort o' heartsome.
> No that they're bonny hills like Moffat hills, na', na',
> ill-shapen sort of things, just like Borunty tatties, awfu'
> puir names too, Shap Fell and Rowland Edge, Hutton
> Roof Crags and Arnside Fell; heard ever onybody
> sich-like names for hills? Naething to fill the mooth;
> man, the Scotch hills jist grap ye in the mooth for a'
> the world like speerits.

As the train crosses into Scotland it become clear that
Andrew cannot live much longer, Jock tells his brother:

> I would hae liket awfu' weel that ye should win to
> Moffat. Man, the rowan trees are a' in bloom, and there's
> a bonny breer upon the corn – aye, ou aye, the reid bogs

are lookin' gran' the year – but Andra', I'll tak ye east
to the auld kirk-yaird, ye'll no' ken onything aboot it,
but we'll hae a heartsome funeral.

There is a curious paradox in this Scotch obsession with
the land. Few nations have suffered so much over their
land or have, today, so little control of their land. At the
present day in Scotland, unlike many other countries,
there is a totally free market in the sale of land: in consequence large tracts of the country are in the possession,
often the absentee possession, of foreign nationals. Of
course, many of these foreign landlords have proved to
be worthy guardians of the land, but many have proved
to be unsympathetic and uninvolved. In either case it
is strange to see people from countries where there
are severe limitations on non-native ownership of
land coming to Scotland and purchasing estates and
properties of great historic, cultural, scenic and
economic importance as if they were no more than a
factory or an office-block. Walter Scott's question :

> Breathes there the man with soul so dead,
> Who never to himself hath said,
> This is my own, my native land!

is hardly likely to be answered in the affirmative by
the Dutch businessman, American oil magnate or Arab
sheik currently found in possession of broad Scottish
acres.

The dispossession of a large part of the Highland
population from their traditional homes in the
Highland Clearances, the struggle of the remnant
population to win enough crofting land and enough
security of tenure to enable them to survive is an oft-
told tale. One telling insight comes from James Boswell's
Journal of a Tour to the Hebrides: writing of his visit to
Skye in 1773 he says:

Mrs. M'Kinnon told me that last year when a ship sailed from Portree for America, the people on shore were almost distracted when they saw their relations go off; they lay down on the ground, tumbled, and tore the grass with their teeth. – This year there was not a tear shed. The people on shore seemed to think that they would soon follow. This indifference is a mortal sign for the country.

A perception shared by his travelling companion, Dr Johnson, who, discussing the evils of emigration and the post-Culloden "settlement" of the Highlands wrote:

To hinder insurrection, by driving away the people, and to govern peaceably, by having no subjects, is an expedient that argues no great profundity of politicks.

One could argue, with some conviction, that our Scottish obsession with the land is a displacement activity to hide the fact that the land, however beautiful, however romantic, is no longer the people's land. Have we, perhaps, idolised "Grannie's Hieland Hame" to conceal the fact that granny no longer has a highland home, that granny was evicted from Strathnaver by Patrick Sellar in 1814, or, to bring matters up to date, that granny can no longer afford to buy a croft-house in Ardnamurchan because such properties are much sought-after as holiday homes and they are consequently priced out of the reach of local people.

Such problems are not new and the need for equity and justice in the land is not new. Four hundred and fifty years ago, Sir David Lyndsay, in his poem *The Dreme* wrote :

Of the Realme of Scotland
Quhen that I had oversene this Regioun,
The quhilk, of nature, is boith gude and fair,
I did propone ane lytill questioun,

Beseikand his the sam for to declare.
Quhat is the cause our boundis bene so bair?
Quod I: or quhate dois mufe our Miserie?
Or quarehof dois proceid our povertie?

After recounting the natural riches and resources of the land and the merits of the people

More fairer peple, nor of gretar ingyne,
Nor of more strength gret dedis tyll indure

the poet concludes, in terms that would appeal to a Strathnaver cottar, a Highland Land Leaguer of the 1890s or an Assynt crofter attempting, in the 1990s to buy the estate on which his croft stands:

So, this is myne conclusion fynall:
Wanting of Justice, polycie, and peace,
Ar cause of thir unhappynes, allace,

It is deficill Riches tylle incres,
Quhare Polycie makith no residence,
And Policey may never have entres,
Bot quhare that Justice dois delygence. . .

A GUID SCOTS TONGUE

The Scots and their Language

"But I'll never find it!"
"Why ever not! You can ask, can't you? You've a
guid Scots tongue in yer heid, haven't you?"

With many similar exchanges, so the older generation were once wont to counsel their offspring.
However, when the self-same offspring went down the
road to school they were apt to receive a very different
message. For there, until comparatively recently, there
were few encouragements to use that other first tongue
which came with varying degrees of naturalness to
youngsters. In fact, there were positive discouragements
– indeed an almost obsessive desire to ban Scots from
the classroom. The belt, or tawse, or Lochgelly, was
used frequently to root out heinous practices like the
use of words like *hoose* or *tatties*, and the public trial
conducted beforehand by someone who, paradoxically,
would not have objected to the Scots word "dominie",
was used as an occasion to deter others from abuses of
the "King's English".

Here is Chris Guthrie, in Lewis Grassic Gibbon's *A
Scots Quair,* with a more mature reflection:

So that was Chris and her reading and schooling, two
Chrisses there were that fought for her heart and

tormented her. You hated the land and the coarse speak
of the folk and learning was brave and fine one day and
the next you'd waken with the peewits crying across the
hills, deep and deep, crying in the heart of you and the
smell of the earth in your face, almost you'd cry for that,
the beauty of it and the sweetness of the Scottish land
and skies. You saw their faces in firelight, father's and
mother's and the neighbours'. . . you wanted the
words they'd known and used, forgotten in the far-off
youngness of their lives, Scots words to tell to your heart,
how they wrung it and held it, the toil of their days and
unendingly their fight. And the next minute that passed
from you, you were English, back to the English words
so sharp and clean and true – for a while, for a while, till
they slid so smooth from your throat you knew the could
never say anything that was worth the saying at all.

Schools nowadays are much more receptive to and
supportive of the "language which children bring to
school" and insofar as that language has a strong
vernacular element and is arguably "Scots", there is a
kind of recognition of it within the school curriculum.
However, that is not always how Scotland's public face
regards certain usages which it deems to be incorrect
or not standard English. Take the recent case of the
Sheriff who held a youth before him in contempt for
answering "aye" to questions to which the sheriff
expected 'yes' or "no". Shades of Lord Braxfield! So,
there is still considerable prejudice in certain quarters
against "common" or "slovenly" speech, or more
especially articulation.

But the fact is that, like Chris Guthrie, many Scots
have a facility of what might be called bilingualism,
which they don't always acknowledge, even to themselves.
They spend much of their lives using an educated Scots
or "Scottish Standard English" which has been purged

of the more extreme Scotticisms, like "aye", but on other occasions they are able to draw upon a fund of idiom and vocabulary and even grammar, which has considerable attractiveness and vigour.

Even when tracing the story of the Scots language back to its earliest surviving fragments, certain turns of phrase turn up that seem distinctively and vividly Scots, and have echoes in modern day speech, as in the use of the word "sore" in this song or chant supposed to have been sung by Scots lasses taunting the enemy in the aftermath of Bannockburn:

> Maidens of Englonde, sore may ye mourn
> For your lemmans ye have lost at Bannockisborne!
> With hevaloghe.
> What wenyth the King of Englande
> So soon to have won Scotland?
> With rumbyloghe.

You may still hear a mother talking about a child "crying sore".

This early Scots was the speech of those people of Scotland and Northern England who spoke a variety of the Germanic tongue which they themselves termed "Inglis" – a variety which (unwillingly) had come under a strong Danish or Norse influence. From the Norse came vigorous words like *gowk* and *breeks* and *lug* and *flit* (in the removal sense) and even, surprisingly, *kilt*. Somewhat later a series of French borrowings began to appear as the Kings of Scots, of Norman-French lineage, established the links which led to the Auld Alliance. At this time, probably, words such as *rammy* and *mavis* and *coup* were adopted, as well as the familiar *caddie, Hogmanay, provost, bailie* and *ashet* (assiette). Two examples, which are almost unchanged from their French forms but have a delightfully different Scots twist to their meanings, are *fash* and *douce*.

Other importations came from the Dutch, including *scone, pinkie* and the contentious *gowf*, and from Latin as well as from the language of that long reviled other face of Scotland – Gaelic. In addition to this recorded history of the languages, the ebb and flow of power politics can be traced through the linguistic patterns of the place-names of Scotland.

So these were some of the ingredients which, by the sixteenth century, had blended together to make a rich, invigorating language, sharing a common ancestry with English but with its own distinctive character and capable of creating a strong literary identity. This was to find expression in the poetry of the "Makars", a term embracing such disparate talents as Dunbar, Henryson and Gavin Douglas. All wrote verse in what was by then a tough, flexible language, which could handle the task of translation from the classical authors, including Douglas's *Aeneid* and Henryson's *Testament of Crisyde*. Dunbar, perhaps the best of these, could also exploit the potential Scots had for "flyting" or abusing, as in his attack here on speakers of Scotland's third language, Erse or Gaelic:

> Then cryit Mahoun for a Hieland padyane;
> Syne ran a fiend to fetch MacFadyen,
> Far northward in a nook;
> Be he the coronach had done shout
> Erschemen so gadderit him about,
> In Hell great room they took
>
> Thae tarmegantis with a tag and tatter,
> Full loud in Ersche begouth to clatter,
> And roup like raven and rook:
> The Devil sa deavit was with their yell,
> That in the deepest pit of Hell
> He smorit them with smoke.

And that was how the Scots language stood when James VI and I , or Jamie the Saxt went south in 1603.

Today, nearly four centuries later, the Makars' work is almost inaccessible to a majority of Scots, and the title of Dunbar's masterpiece, *The Lament for the Makaris*, seems strangely prophetic.

Perhaps it is not as bad as all that. There were such irreversible political and religious changes in the intervening period that the linguistic changes are not to be wondered at, but, as has already been argued, there remains for many Scots a sense in which they are bilingual. And this can be detected, not just in their vocabulary, but in their grammar and idiom. It can be observed most easily, however in the way they speak, rather than in the way they write.

Take for example, verbs such as *want* or *need*, which have peculiarly Scottish constructions – *the dog's needing out for a walk, the windows are needing washed*. Also, the endearing usages such as *I'm away out* or *that's me away then* or *where do you stay?* or, *you missed yourself!*

So there are benefits to be had from bilingualism, although the more usual view of it is that it betrays a sort of uncertainty about role and identity. Some would argue that it this uncertainty is connected with the well-known Scottish guilt complex and with the kind of fumbling inarticulacy which descends upon Scots when they are asked to contribute to vox pops or press interviews – when the the "ye kens" and "an" "ats" and "thingmys" come pouring forth. Isn't there a paradox here, though?

Compared with the ease, or blandness, of expression of the typical Englishman yes, there is a halting quality about the Scotsman's discourse – but transpose the same Scot to a situation where his "dander is up" or he is "goin' his mile" or he is in the midst of a good-going argument or debate and the words come with greater facility, and the charge of inarticulacy seems less justified. Hence the quite remarkable "world-class" performance of university debaters on the international stage or the kind of polemic or "tirravee" employed by people like Billy Connolly, in the manner, perhaps, of the flytings of earlier days.

One of the long line of Scots fictional characters who could be said to "go his dinger" is Neil Munro's Erchie. In 1922 Erchie gives this apocalyptic view of the future of cities.

> The streets in the middle o' Gleska were laid oot for a population no' the size o'Greenock. The great mistake was that they werena made o' kahouchy as lang as Menzies's buses and the horse had the cairryin' traffic there was nae great inconvenience to the foot passenger; he could stop in the middle o' the street an' tie his laces, and there wasna ony need for an ambulance. But any kahouchy quality the streets had vanished when the tram-rail and the motor came in vogue. Nae human ingenuity noo can widen them to accommodate safely what's expected o' them. In the past ten years the population's risen a quarter o' a million; the traffic's speeded up at least four times what it used to be when the horse was bloomin'; and twenty years from noo, when everybody has a motor-car, ye'll see some fun!

The jaundiced eye of the English novelist, Anthony Powell, finds this facility somewhat less endearing and makes these sardonic comments:

> Books writ for Scotchmen and for Scotchmen writ,
> Devoid of Humour and divorced from Wit,
> Well-fitted Caledonians to beguile',
> In content dull; cacophonous in style.
> A Basin! Quick! Ah Me! The Stomach turns!
> The Prose of B-RR—, and the Verse of B-RNS!
> > *Caledonia*

It may be that this heightening of expression that we are arguing for is a consequence of the sudden appearance of the demotic in the middle of otherwise stilted discourse, but it is equally likely that the mingling of the two languages – and we believe that Scots still is distinctive enough to be described as a language – produces the added vigour of expression. A gey potent mixture!

Turning now to the way that Scotland's great writers since the Makars have used Scots: there is no substantial body of prose works in Scots, even from the time when it was the tongue of most Lowlanders. This is commonly said to due to the fact that the greatest single influence on prose was the "Good Book" and the translations of scriptures favoured by the Scots Protestants from the Reformation were, firstly, the Geneva Bible and then the Authorised Version. The "King James Bible" was magnificent language, with an immense impact on the written and spoken word in the succeeding centuries, but it was not *in* Scots, even though it was authorised by a speaker *of* Scots.

As spoken Scots declined in the seventeenth and eighteenth centuries – a process strengthened by the custom among leading families of sending their sons to England or abroad for their education – so it was replaced by English in almost all everyday prose forms and in most of literature except vernacular poetry. (Burns wrote only one letter in Scots – the ambiguities of his attitude to English in his verse are well known. Perhaps a Freudian would suggest that Scots was what Burns unconsciously repressed, since obviously there was little wrong with his libido.) The tradition of literary prose, in the sense of texts written almost exclusively in Scots, had never been strong anyway, but towards the end of the eighteenth century some writers began to look for ways to weave Scots into otherwise English narratives. Not James Boswell though.

Even if Boswell probably spoke Scots at home in Auchinleck and was at other times an enthusiastic patriot, he would only go a very little way in support of the old language:

> Let me give my countrymen of North-Britain an advice not to aim at absolute perfection in this respect. . . A studied and factitious pronunciation, which requires perpetual attention and imposes perpetual constraint, is exceedingly disgusting. A small intermixture of provincial peculiarities may, perhaps, have an agreeable effect, as the notes of different birds concur in the harmony of the grove, and please more than if they were all exactly alike.

James Hogg and later John Galt went much further in trying to forge an English prose style with strong Scots elements, but it was Walter Scott who had the most complex and interesting approach. His method was to introduce Scots characterisation into his novels, and as they developed through the great series with Scottish themes and settings, beginning with *Waverley* and including *The Antiquary* and *Heart of Midlothian* and Redgauntlet, the Scots element gradually grew until the dialogue of the characters like Andrew Fairservice and Meg Merrilies and Dominie Sampson were more than just comic relief and became integral to the development of the themes and protagonists of the action.

Andrew Fairservice in *Rob Roy* here makes some observations on the 1707 Union, which of course indirectly was a contributing factor in the decline of Scots.

> When we had a Scotch Parliament, says I (and deil rax their thrapples that reft us o't), they sate dousely down and made laws for a haill country and kinrick, and never fashed their beards about things that were competent to the judge ordinar' o' the bounds; but I think, said I, that

if ae kail-wife pou'd aff her neigbour's mutch, they wad
hae the twasome o' them into the Parliament House o'
Lunnun.

The great pity was that Scott never went so far as to
attempt a novel entirely in Scots. Neither did Stevenson,
although *Weir of Hermiston* has the same kind of rich
fusion of Scots idiom and dialogue. Moreover, *Thrawn
Janet*, a short story, is complete in this sense, apart
from a brief preface:

> She was nae great speaker; folk usually let her gang
> her ain gate, an' she let them gang theirs, wi' neither
> Fair-guid-e'en nor Fair-guid-day; but when she buckled
> to, she had a tongue to deave the miller. Up she got,
> an' there wasna an auld story in Ba'weary but she gart
> somebody lowp for it that day; they couldna say ae
> thing but she could say twa to it.

Then Grassic Gibbon gave the dialogue of his characters
a new, almost rejuvenated regional thrust, and, as we
saw, picked up strong Scots rhythms and intonations in
his "English" narrative. The new minister in "Sunset
Song" in his eulogy for the Fallen of Kinraddie in the
First World War seems more pessimistic.

> It was the old Scotland that perished then, and we may
> believe that never again will the old speech and the old
> songs, the old curses and the old benedictions, rise but
> with alien effort to our lips.

The Scots Renaissance of the twentieth century has
been mainly concentrated on verse, although regional
prose writings, especially from the North-East, have
had some success. However, in closing here is some
speculation about what the state of the Scots language
might have been, had events not taken the turn they did.
If there had been no Union, if there had been no King

James Bible, if the Scots language had been effortless and with no hint of an obsession about it, could we all have been writing and speaking like this?

> Gin I speak wi the tungs o men an angels, but hae nae luve in my hairt, I am no nane better nor dunnerin bress or a ringing cymbal
>
> W. L Lorimer *The New Testament in Scots*

NOT PROVEN

The Scots and the Law

*O*ne of the central articles of Scottish faith is that
the Scottish legal system is of peculiar excellence
and enjoys a mysterious superiority to that found in all
other jurisdictions (which, of course, chiefly means
England). This view is held both by lawyers and
by a lay public which takes a strange and perhaps
irrational delight in the peculiarities of Scots law and its
terminology. That this is not a new phenomenon is
demonstrated by Walter Scott's depiction of Bartoline
Saddletree, harness-maker and amateur of the law, in
The Heart of Midlothian. Saddletree was a habitual
attender at the law courts and an assiduous reader of
legal textbooks which he sadly failed to understand but
with which he nonetheless impressed or infuriated his
unfortunate neighbours and family.

> Whoy, there are two sorts of *murdrum*, or *murdragium*,
> or what you *populariter et vulgariter* call murther. I
> mean there are many sorts; for there's your *murthrum*
> *per vigilias et insidias*, and your *murthrum* under trust.

He goes on to expound on the charge of child-murder
being faced by Effie Deans:

> The crime is rather a favourite of the law, this species
> of murther being one of its ain creation.

A pleasingly cynical view of the law and its practitioners is, however, expressed by Mrs. Saddletree:

> Then if the law makes murders, the law should be hanged for them; or if they wad hang a lawyer instead, the country wad find nae fault.

The most obvious thing that everyone knows about Scots Law, and the reason for much of its obsessive hold on the Scottish people, is that not only is it different but that its difference is protected and institutionalised in the 1707 Act of Union. Article 18 of this states:

> . . .that no alteration be made in Laws which concern private Right, except for the evident utility of the Subjects within Scotland.

while Article 19 had decreed:

> That the Court of Session, or College of Justice, do after the Union, and notwithstanding thereof, remain in all time coming within Scotland, as it is now constituted by the Laws of that Kingdom, and with the same Authority and Privileges as before the Union. . . and that the Court of Justiciary do also after the Union, and notwithstanding thereof, remain in all time coming within Scotland. . .

The Court of Session had been founded by James V in 1532 as a permanent and professional supreme court – in the words of the Act as:

> . . .ane college of cunning and wise men for the administracioun of Justice.

It is difficult to avoid the conclusion that this tenacious survival and the independence of the Scots legal system is at the root of much of the Scottish love affair with the law. The Law as an institution has come to act in a sense as a substitute for nationhood. Just as the General

Assembly of the Church of Scotland continues to attract a remarkable degree of public and media attention in what is repeatedly (if inaccurately) described as a post-Christian culture because it has come to carry a symbolic and representational role in a stateless nation, so the law has become a touchstone of Scottishness and a symbol of differentiation.

The uniqueness of Scottish law, a blend of the Continental Civil Law system and the English Common Law, of course predates the Act of Union. The survival of the Scottish system at the Act of Union would seem to owe much to the codification of Scots Law, and the creation of a coherent intellectual basis for it, in works like Stair's *Institutions of the Laws of Scotland* published in 1681. That Scots had a "guid conceit of themselves" and of their legal system even then can be demonstrated from Sir James Dalrymple of Stair's "Dedication to the King" in the first edition:

> . .. the law of this kingdom hath attained to so great
> perfection, that it may, without arrogance, be compared
> with the laws of any of our neighbouring nations. . .

Dalrymple also asserted that old Scottish principle – empirical pragmatism:

> . . .we do always prefer the sense, to the subtility, of
> law, and do seldom trip by niceties or formalities.

The underlying principles and roots of Scottish law which distinguish it from the English system are not perhaps widely understood. What is more popularly understood is, in a sense, the surface manifestations of difference – the Not Proven verdict, the fifteen strong jury and the requirement for corroboration in criminal cases, the 110 day rule. Understanding of a legal system might perhaps be thought to be quite a long way from a popular commitment to it, or indeed to its qualifying as a national obsession. However both as a surrogate for nationhood and as a central part of Scottish life over the centuries the law can surely, with some justice, be described as a Scotch obsession.

One of the elements which certainly contributed to the centrality of the law in Scottish consciousness was the familiarity of the population with the practitioners and dispensers of the law. In Edinburgh before the building of the New Town everyone had at least a nodding acquaintance with writers, advocates and judges. In the eighteenth century many of the Court of Session judges walked, in full judicial dress, from their homes in the closes and wynds of the Old Town to Parliament House, although one, Lord Monboddo (1714-1799), was apt, in wet weather, to send his wig to Court by sedan chair in wet weather while he slaistered through the mud and glaur of the Edinburgh streets. The close proximity in which all classes lived made the law and its practitioners a familiar part of everyday life even if all citizens did not have a Bartoline Saddletree's obsessive interest in its minutiae.

It might also be felt that the survival of heritable jurisdiction, the right of landowners to try all cases short of those specifically reserved to the Crown – a right which, however attenuated in practice, survived until 1748, integrated the law into society and everyday life in a way which a more centralised and governmentally organised system could not have done.

Another element in the growth of the law to its central place in national life was the dominance of lawyers, and in particular of the members of the Faculty of Advocates, in the social and intellectual life of post-Union Scotland. It is no isolated chance that the creator of Bartoline Saddletree was himself an advocate, a Sheriff-Depute and a Clerk of the Court of Session. The legal profession provided Scotland with writers such as

James Boswell, Henry MacKenzie, and at the end of the nineteenth century Robert Louis Stevenson. The Faculty of Advocates was even to provide the country with the origins of its National Library. In the absence of a Parliament and a higher administration the law attracted a social and intellectual elite and acted as a surrogate field for political conflict.

For these and other reasons in the great age of the Scottish Enlightenment and on into the nineteenth century lawyers and, in particular, the judiciary had a much greater impact on the public than they do today and this has doubtless contributed to the place of the law in the national consciousness. Few non-lawyers today could name the Senators of the College of Justice and – without wishing to run the risk of committing the grave offence of "murmuring a judge" – it is probably safe and true to observe that today's Court of Session judges seem a somewhat colourless group compared to their eighteenth century forebears. Dean Ramsay recounts the following behaviour indulged in by Francis Garden, Lord Gardenstone (1721-1793) :

> He took a young pig as a pet, and it became quite tame,
> and followed him about like a dog. At first the animal
> shared his bed, but when, growing up to advanced
> swinehood, it became unfit for such companionship,
> he had it to sleep in his room, in which he made a
> comfortable couch for it of his own clothes.

This could be seen as a slightly extreme version of the 1980's fashion for the Vietnamese Pot-Bellied Pig as a fashionable pet but present day aspirants to the judicial benches are probably not recommended to go to bed with a Tamworth sow. Equally certainly contemporary judges are unlikely to come out with the views of a Lord Braxfield (1722-1799), such as:

> Hang a thief when he is young, and he'll no' steal
> when he is auld.

or his remark to a prisoner:

> Ye're a verra clever chiel, man, but ye wad be nane
> the waur o' a hanging.

whatever their private views. Braxfield has had a bad press for his undoubtedly partial and oppressive handling of the sedition trials of Muir of Huntershill and the other radicals in 1793; his positive qualities are less often remarked. Robert McQueen, Lord Braxfield, was the grandson of a gardener to the Earl of Selkirk – a somewhat unlikely background for the eighteenth-century Scottish judiciary – most of whose grandfathers were more likely to have owned a landed estate than have worked on one. Braxfield was the outstanding intellect of the Scottish bench of his day and a devoted supporter of the Scottish language and Scottish ways and a pungent critic of creeping Anglicisation.

It was Braxfield, of course, who provided Stevenson with the model for his Lord Hermiston in *The Weir of Hermiston*. Another manifestation of the Scots obsession with law and lawyers is the use that our writers have made of the law. *The Weir of Hermiston* is a love story, but its opening pages includes a confrontation over capital punishment between the austere, autocratic, but not entirely unsympathetic, figure of Hermiston and his impulsive, romantic, son Archie. The old judge tells his son, who has publicly objected to the hanging of one Duncan Jopp:

> I was glad to get Jopp haangit, and what for would
> I pretend I wasna?

Stevenson was to use the law, in the shape of a famous Scottish murder case, the slaying of Colin Campbell of

Glenure – the Appin Murder – as the point of departure for *Kidnapped*. In its sequel, *Catriona*, the trial of James Stewart of the Glen for Campbell's shooting is featured. This trial was memorably, and quite fairly, described by Alan Breck Stewart in *Kidnapped* in the following way:

> This is a Campbell that's been killed. Well, it'll be tried in Inverara, the Campbell's head place, with fifteen Campbells in the jury-box, and the biggest Campbell of all (and that's the Duke) sitting cocking on the bench.

The young and naive David Balfour (who was to become a lawyer himself) suggests that the Duke of Argyll was a wise and honest nobleman and a fair trial was thus assured. To which Alan responds, with commendable realism:

> . . . the man's a Whig, nae doubt; but I would never deny he was a good chieftain to his clan. And what would the clan think if there was a Campbell shot and naebody hanged, and their own chief the Justice General?

Incidentally Braxfield/Hermiston illuminates another feature of the Scots legal world that may well have influenced the way that the general populace regarded it – the survival of a characteristically Scotch idiom and accent. When other parts of the "establishment" were becoming increasingly Anglicised, elements of the judiciary and the legal profession seem to have largely retained their Scottishness. As Lord Braxfield's reported remarks indicate, this Scottishness was sometimes retained to a marked degree. The well known story of John Clerk (1757-1832), later raised to the Bench as Lord Eldin, demonstrates this attractive persistence. Clerk was pleading an appeal case in the House of Lords which hinged on his client's right to the use of a mill stream. Clerk argued in a broad Scots accent that:

. . .the watter had rin that way for forty years. Indeed naebody kenn'd how long, and why should his client be deprived of the watter.

The Lord Chancellor made sport of the Scottish advocate's pronunciation by asking:

Mr Clerk do you spell water in Scotland with two t's?

To which the offended Clerk splendidly responded:

Na, my Lord, we dinna spell watter wi' two t's but we spell mainners wi' twa n's.

Which is perhaps an appropriate point to suggest another reason for the law's grip on the Scottish imagination – a rich vocabulary of legal terminology. We know much of the law's delays, but somehow it softens the blow of a delay in passing judgement when the judge wishes time to consider the matter if the judicial action is graced with the mellifluous term "makes avizandum". It would almost be a pleasure to face a charge of "stouthrief" – theft with violence – or "hamesucken" – assaulting a person in their own home. One Scots judge, Lord Eskgrove (1724 – 1804), had to deal with a case of hamesucken and, sentencing the miscreants, concluded his review of their crimes:

All this you did; and God preserve us! just when they were sitten doon to their denner!

– which shows a proper judicial sense of concern for family life and the sanctity of meal times.

The Scottish belief in the virtues of their legal system – a belief which extends from the arrangements for the purchase of houses to majority verdicts – has grown by comparison with that of their neighbours. Its standing has been reinforced in recent years by the various cases of wrongful conviction which have plagued the English criminal system. The Scots Law's insistence on corroboration has been claimed to protect against erroneous identification and forensic evidence. The Scottish system, with its insistence that no one can be held in custody on criminal charges for more than 110 days unless the trial has commenced (an astonishingly liberal enactment of the Scottish Parliament in 1701), is seen to avoid the unacceptably long periods of detention without trial found elsewhere. The Scottish system of prosecution in criminal cases by an agency independent of the police – the Procurator Fiscal or the Crown Office – has in recent years been copied in England by the creation of the Crown Prosecution Service. One of the undoubted glories of the Scottish legal system, and a justifiable cause for pride, has been the availability of free legal representation in criminal cases. James I in 1425 enacted legislation for the appointment of a:

. . . lele and wyse advocate. . .

for anyone unable to defend himself or employ a lawyer. For centuries in England those accused of felonies were bereft of legal aid, while in Scotland the services of a panel of members of the Faculty of Advocates appointed as counsel for the poor were at the disposal of all of restricted means.

The appointment, in 1987, of a Scottish lawyer, James Mackay, Lord Mackay of Clashfern, as Lord Chancellor and as such head of the English judicial and court system, could be seen as a final vote of confidence in Scots law.

Not, of course, that Scots law has escaped scandal and controversy – or charges of wrongful conviction. Indeed in the present century from Oscar Slater to Paddy Meehan there have been notable cases which would not bear close scrutiny of their procedures and outcomes.

And of course there is Not Proven. Opinions vary on this, the third verdict open to Scottish juries – Walter Scott described it in his Journal as:

> . . . that bastard verdict, Not proven. . . One who is not proven guilty is innocent in the eye of the law.

Others have seen it as a way of saying:

> You did it but we can't prove it – so don't do it again!

There are active moves afoot to remove the "not proven" option – moves which are being equally vigorously resisted. A simple choice of verdicts, "proven" or "not proven", can in fact be seen as strictly logical – a jury can reasonably be asked whether a case is proved or not proved. To say a person is not guilty may be seen as infringing on the prerogatives of the Almighty!

Everyone knows of the not proven verdict as a peculiarly Scottish device, and cherishes it or disdains it accordingly. What is less well known is the history of the verdict. Originally juries were asked to declare an accused "guilty" or "not guilty". In the reign of Charles II this was changed to finding a verdict on the facts presented of "proven" or "not proven". In 1728 Robert Dundas of Arniston was defending Carnegie of Finhaven on the charge of murdering the Earl of Strathmore. The killing had taken place by mistake in a drunken brawl. However Carnegie had clearly killed Strathmore and if the jury found this fact "proven" then Dundas's client was doomed. Dundas persuaded the court to return to the older verdict of "not guilty" and his client was freed and the three possible verdicts began to co-exist. Not proven is often spoken of as the "Scottish third verdict" – but one could with equal logic describe "not guilty" as the "third verdict".

What the future of this Scotch obsession will be is hard to say. There is a steady erosion of the individuality of Scots Law by the increasingly prevalent practice in Parliament of tacking on Scottish legislation to English Bills. On the positive side it has been argued that Scots Law, standing as it does midway between the English Common Law tradition and the European Roman Civil Law tradition, may find its position strengthened by the increasingly important part that European Community legislation plays in our affairs nowadays. Lord Belhaven, opposing the Act of Union in the Scots Parliament in 1706, displayed a classically Scotch Obsession with the law and the threat the Union would pose:

> I think I see our Learned Judges laying aside their Practiques and Decisions, studying the Common Law of England, gravelled with Certioraries, *Nisi prius's*, Writs of Errors, Verdicts indovar, *Ejectione firmae*, Injunctions, Demurrs, &c, and frighted with Appeals and Avocations, because of the new Regulations and Rectifications they may meet with.

Many of Belhaven's other fears were well-founded, but the Law has proved more resilient than he feared and has survived nearly three centuries with most of its features intact.

CALEDONIA STERN AND WILD

The Scots and Literature

Scots have a well-founded reputation for taciturnity and inarticulateness. It is somewhat curious, therefore, that they also have a deep affection for the written and spoken word, and consequently for literature, that is so strong that it almost amounts to obsession. A possible reason for this might be the long history of scriptural knowledge and religious disputation in this country. If the Bible is literature, it was for centuries the literature of the people. More than that, there were many who held the "good book" or "Scripture" to be as dear to them as their own lives. The seventeenth-century Covenanters went into battle clutching the Bible. Burns's picture of the toil-worn father in *The Cottar's Saturday Night* shows him with the Scriptures at the very centre of his and his family's life:

> The Sire turns o'er , with patriarchal grace,
> The big ha'-Bible, ance his father's pride:
> His bonnet reverently is laid aside,
> His lyart haffets wearing thin and bare;
> These strains that once did sweet in Zion glide,
> He wales a portion with judicious care;
> "And let us worship God!" he says with solemn air.

To be less apocalyptic, there is ample evidence of Scots'

love of books. One need only think of the history of the miners' libraries at Wanlockhead and Leadhills to see the enthusiasm that the lead-miners of the mid-eighteenth century had for books, reading and self-improvement. As a great nineteenth-century Scots writer, Thomas Carlyle, observed:

> On all sides, are we not driven to the conclusion that,
> of the things which man can do or make here below, by
> far the most momentous, wonderful and worthy are the
> things we call Books! those poor bits of rag-paper with
> black ink on them;- from the Daily Newspaper to the
> sacred Hebrew BOOK, what have they not done, what
> are they not doing!

And the Scottish appetite for the printed word continues, with that staple of the Sunday breakfast-table, the *Sunday Post*, featuring in the Guinness Book of Records for its achievement of the highest market penetration of any national newspaper.

As to writers or other literary figures themselves, Scotland has a pantheon of famous individuals as impresssive as any nation of its size. The late Alexander Scott, a poet himself and an unforgettable influence on a generation of students of Scottish literature at Glasgow University, defined the nation's literary tradition and called the roll of its famous names. They included the inventor of the historical novel, Walter Scott; Robert Burns, one of the world's two or three greatest lyric poets, Boswell, the greatest of biographers, and Hogg and Stevenson, the progenitors of the psychological novel. All have an assured place in world literature.

To begin with "The Wizard Of the North", the years have not been kind to his particular brand of alchemy, and Walter Scott's work does not have the same popularity today that it had at the height of his fame at the beginning of the nineteenth century. So the quality of his work is less appreciated, but there is no doubt about its quantity. Scott certainly himself exhibited obsessive literary endeavours. In an age of workaholics, his prodigious labours to extricate himself from financial ruin after the collapse of his publishers were only rivalled by Balzac. In the early decades of the century, Scott feverishly wrote novel after novel, to growing acclaim at home and abroad. He initially won his international reputation from the sprawling verse romances, largely historical in theme, like *Marmion* and *The Lay of the Last Minstrel*. The memorising of great chunks of these poems, like the following from the *Minstrel* was for a while *de rigueur* throughout the English speaking world:

> O Caledonia! stern and wild
> Meet nurse for a poetic child!
> Land of brown heath and shaggy wood,
> Land of the mountain and the flood.
> Land of my sires! What mortal hand
> Can e'er untie the filial band
> That knits me to thy rugged strand!

Scott then carried his readers over into a great sequence of novels with Scottish settings, beginning with *Waverley* and ending with *Redgauntlet*. All drew extensively on the wealth of Scottish myth, folk tale and legend, and to this he added a powerful, almost obsessive vision of history as an imaginative source of inspiration, an educative force, and a means of shaping the relatively new literary form of the novel. Scott's followers and imitators became legion – the U.S. Presidential Anthem *Hail to the Chief* comes from *The Lady of the Lake*, and *The Bride of Lammermoor* and *The Fair Maid of Perth* are just two of his works to inspire operatic composers, while as a novelist his influence can be traced to Tolstoy. Mark Twain suggested that Scott's over-glamourised Romantic view of chivalry and aristocracy was so pervasive in the American South that it helped to precipitate the Civil War. In Scotland his most successful heirs in the historical tradition are probably Stevenson and Munro.

So Scott has been credited with the invention of one important literary *genre*, but the immense popularity of his books and their deep sense of place also contributed to the development of a social phenomenon, which has turned into an obsession – the modern love-affair with travel and tourism. Certainly tourists today don't come crowding to the Trossachs with *Waverley* in hand as many did in its author's day, although recent filmic versions of Scottish history might just revive these enthusiams. Certainly, too, Scott was intent in communicating his own love of Scotland's landscape and scenery, events and people, to as wide an audience as possible. In *Rob Roy* he describes Loch Lomond:

> This noble lake, boasting innumerable beautiful
> islands, of every varying form and outline which fancy
> can frame – its northern extremity narrowing until it
> is lost among dusky and retreating mountains, while,
> gradually widening as it extends to the southward,
> it spreads its base around the indentures and
> promontories of a fair and fertile land – offers one
> of the most surprising, beautiful, and sublime
> spectacles in nature.

Splendid advertising copy! More than this, however. In an aside to the reader, Scott says something which could almost represent a slogan for modern tourism and its compelling desire to travel ever further, in search of more experience:

> I will spare you the attempt to describe what you would
> hardly comprehend without going to see it

This is in a way reminiscent of Robert Burns's "Humble Petition of Bruar Water", when the waterfall claims:

> I am, altho' I say it mysel'
> Worth gaun a mile to see.

In reaching the matter of Robert Burns, "Scotland's National Poet", "The Bard", and similar descriptions, we do face a national obsession of the first degree. "There was a lad was born in Kyle", and it is his laddishness, or to be fairer, his charm, which is the first remarkable feature of Scotland's infatuation with Burns. It is a charm which was immediately apparent to his contemporaries. Walter Scott, after a meeting with him, remembered his expressive eye(s):

> It literally glowed. I never saw such another eye in a human head, though I have seen the most distinguished men in my time.

But the infatuation goes deeper. The love that Burns seems to have inspired in the men and especially the women of the eighteenth century, was certainly returned by the man himself, and besides his many particular affections, this was a generalised love, encompassing the future as well as the present:

> For a' that, and a' that,
> It's comin' yet for a' that,
> That man to man, the warld o'er,
> Shall brothers be for a' that!

This mutual love, or infatuation, has grown over the years, and, as has often been remarked, has reached the status of a cult. Many debunking journalists seize the annual opportunity to ridicule the institution or ritual of the Burns Supper, and there is, admittedly, something ridiculous about the way the regulars on the "Burns Circuit" go traipsing round dozens of wee halls every

January and February. Take the ill-judged way in which the wonderful "Address to the Haggis" is sometimes delivered by those who "tear a passion to tatters, to rags, to split the ears of the groundlings", as Burns, who loved his Shakespeare, might have observed if he had lived to see it.

There is, of course, an echo of Shakespearean "bardolatry" in the cult of Burns although there is certainly a marked contrast between the Scottish welter of Burns Clubs and Burns Suppers and the remarkable absence of any form of popular celebration of Shakespeare, Milton or Wordsworth. There are many who argue that the ordinary people of Scotland identify more closely with and know more about their "bard" than the English do about theirs. Perhaps, but it is sometimes mixed with a kind of uncritical chauvinism. The famous occasion comes to mind, when, after the first performance of Home's (long forgotten) tragedy, *Douglas*, the audience came spilling out of the Canongate Theatre and someone called out triumphantly, in the manner of a football fan, "Whaur's yer Wullie Shakespeare noo?".

How well do the Scots know their Burns, then? Neil Munro's Duffy, in the "Erchie" humorous stories is perhaps not a representative example. This extract from "A Bet on Burns" also alludes to some of the politically incorrect features of bardolatry. Duffy the coalman calls round to borrow a copy of Burns from Erchie:

"I'm wantin' to learn a sang, for I'm gaun to the Haggis Club in the Mull of Kintyre Vaults on Monday if I'm spared."

"Are ye indeed!" said Erchie drily. "Ye'll be takin' the new wife wi' ye?"

"No fears o' me", said Duffy. "Wha ever heard o' a wife at a Burns meetin'?"

"Oh! I divna ken onything aboot it," said Erchie: "I

thocht maybe the weemen were gaun to thae things
nooadays. . . It's a droll thing aboot Burns that though
the weemen were sae ta'en up wi' him when he was
leevin', they're no awfu' keen on him noo that he's deid.
There'll be thoosands o' men hurrayin' Burns on Monday
nicht in a' pairts o' then world, and eatin' haggis till
they're no' weel, but I'll bet ye their wifes is no' there.

Later, Duffy tells about another bet he has made:

"There's a chap yonder at the coal hill thrieps doon
my throat Burns didna write `Dark Lochnagar'."
    "Hoo much is the bet?"
    "Hauf-a-croon."
    "Then sell yin o' yer horses and pey the money, for
ye've lost the bet. Burns had nae grudge against his
countrymen. They did him nae harm. . . In fact, he
never wrote 'Dark Lochnagar' at a'. It was put oot by
anither firm in the same trade, ca'd Byron."

And when Duffy refers to another popular image of
Burns, as debauchee: "A gey wild chap, Burns!"
"Maybe no' that awfu' wild," said Erchie. "Ye're aye
harpin' on the wild. Burns was like a man takin' a
daunder oot in a country road on a fine nicht: he kept
his een sae much on the stars that sometimes he tripped
in the sheuch."

"Man, ye should be doon at theHaggis Club on
Monday and propose the toast.'
    "I'm better whaur I am," said Erchie; "the best Burns
Club a man can hae is a weel-thumbed copy o' the
poems and a wife that can sing `Ye Banks and Braes'
like oor Jinnet."

Thus demonstrating the way in which the "copy o' the
poems" has in a sense replaced his cottar's "ha' Bible" in
the homes of later generations and as nice evidence as
you could get that Burns has the securest place that any

poet ever had in the hearts of a people – except perhaps for Pushkin in the hearts of Russians. Edwin Muir, in "Burns and Popular Poetry" put it this way:

> The national poet of Scotland is too conventional a term
> for him; the poet of the Scottish people is better, for all
> claim him. And by the people I do not mean merely the
> ploughman and the factory worker and the grocer's
> assistant, but the lawyer, the business man, the minister,
> the bailie – all that large class of Scotsmen who are not
> very interested in literature, nor very cultivated, and
> who know little poetry outside the poetry of Burns. It
> is these who have fashioned the popular image of Burns;
> and this is what really happens when a poet is taken
> into the life of a people. He moulds their thoughts and
> feelings; but they mould his too, sometimes long after
> he is dead.

Burns was arguably the greatest lyric poet. He was also a supreme satirist, but before this turns into an Immortal Memory, let us turn to consider the role that Burns cast for himself, but never played: Burns the dramatist. At the same time, there needs to be some reference to the strange case of the Scottish literary tradition which never was. Or rather, was strangled at birth.

The story of the drama in Scotland is indeed one of early promise which has never been fulfilled. Things got off to such a splendid start. In the year 1540, considerably in advance of any comparable production south of the Border, Sir David Lyndsay's *Ane Pleasant Satire of the Thrie Estaitis* was first performed for James V's court at Linlithgow and seems to have created a sensation. With its witty and satirical view of the three estates of the realm, comic interludes and innovative staging, this promised to become the first flowering of a new kind of drama, and in Scottish soil moreover. It was soon blighted.

Deceit: Devotion, Sapience and Discretion -
We three may rule this region.
We shall find mony crafty things
For to beguile a hundred kings!
For thou [to Falsehood] can richt weel
    crack and clatter
And I shall feign, and thou shall flatter.

Flatterie: But I wald have, ere we depairtit,
A drink to make us better heartit.

Deceit: Weel said. By Him that herryit hell,
I was even thinkan that mysel'!

The earlier achievements of the Makars, of Dunbar, Douglas and Henryson had been to give authority and status to the Scots language as a suitable vehicle for poetic expression. Poetry, as well as the infant drama, was to wilt in the cold wind that blew from nearly two centuries of religious turmoils, when the religious obsession held sway. However, poetry did eventually revive, with Fergusson and others. The drama, though, could be said to have never recovered. It would be many years before plays of any kind were staged again in Scotland. Worse, the ability to write great theatre seems to have eluded all of Scotland's finest authors, although many have tried. Barrie probably would be the closest thing we have to a great playwright, at least in terms of his contemporary popularity and stylistic influence.

Burns himself never got beyond writing some prologues, much as he loved the theatre, and believed, like others before and since, that Scotland's story was the stuff of drama:

There's themes enow in Caledonian story
Would show the Tragic Muse in a' her glory.
Is there no daring bard will rise, and tell
How glorious Wallace stood, how, hapless, fell?

O for a Shakespeare or an Otway scene
To draw the lovely, hapless Scottish Queen!
Vain all th'omnipotence of female charms
'Gainst headlong, ruthless, mad Rebellion's arms:
She fell, but fell with spirit truly Roman,
To glut the vengeance of a rival woman
  Prologue for Mr Sutherland on his benefit night.

And of course the story of Mary, Queen of Scots, ("from an idea by Robert Burns"!) has attracted Schiller and many other playwrights.

It might be said that the great Scottish writers, instead of writing plays, brought their repressed theatrical sense to bear upon their novels and verse and other writings and infused them with a strong dramatic element. One thinks of *The Jolly Beggars* in this context, but arguably the outstanding "dramatic" theme is the characteristically Scottish idea of the "Divided Self", which appears as a continuous thread running through the literature of the last couple of centuries.

The notion of divided personality, of man at war with himself, with its roots in the tortured Calvinist conscience, is found in many works such as in James Hogg's *Confessions of a Justified Sinner*, and *The Strange Case of Dr Jekyll and Mr Hyde*, by Robert Louis Stevenson.

Hogg's magnificent psychological study, written in 1824, with the character of Robert Wringhim and his evil, Faust-like doppelganger, Gil-Martin, has enjoyed a critical revival in the twentieth century and perhaps influenced Stevenson. But it is *Jekyll and Hyde*, of course, which has had an enormous impact right round the world, and has become synonymous with horrific tales of "split personality". Based on Edinburgh's own Deacon Brodie, it has led to a whole flood of plays, films and books, which seek to recapture Stevenson's supremely dramatic combination of opposites and unpeeling of psychological layers.

And finally, Boswell, the greatest of biographers, who is always remembered as living in Doctor Johnson's shadow, and for many years scarcely existed as a distinct literary figure in his own right. The twentieth century has in a sense reclaimed him since the discovery of a whole mountain of strongly personal journals and other papers revealed an unsuspected private Boswell, a Boswell who also turns out to have had a "secret life". He really is a very familiar kind of figure in modern eyes – an extremely complex, or if you like, "mixed-up" character. The frequent advice to himself contained in the diaries, and his reaction to meeting some Scottish aquaintances in London:

> To tell the plain truth, I was vexed at their coming. For
> to see just the plane *hamely* Fife family hurt my grand
> ideas of London. Besides, I was now upon a plan of
> studying polite reserved behaviour, which is the only
> way to keep up dignity of character.

does suggest a truly Jekyll and Hyde-like split personality. Perhaps, with this and with his strong streak of determination, he is the quintessential Scotsman?

A WEE THING CANNY

The Scots and Money

Did they remain among such unthaw'd Latitudes,
And *Scot* with *Scot* alone exchanged his Platitudes,
Travellers but few would mark their stinted *Bonhomie*,
And smile to see each finicking Œconomy
Alack! They ever stream through ENGLAND'S door
To batten on the Rich, and grind the Poor,
With furtive Eye and eager, clutching hand
They pass like *Locusts* through the Southern Land:
And line their purses with the yellow Gold,
Which for each Scotchman, London's pavements hold,

This extract from the twentieth century English novelist Anthony Powell's mock-Augustan denunciation of Scotland and the Scotch, *Caledonia*, conveniently sums up a commonly held view of the Scots and money – mean at home and avaricious abroad.

Powell is hardly the first outside observer to suggest a tendency to meanness in the Scottish character. The zoologist and traveller, Thomas Pennant, in his *Tour in Scotland, 1769*, has reached Aberdeen and observes of that city:

The East and West churches are under the same roof; for the *North Britons* observe œconomy even in their religion. . .

It is, however, salutary to note that the American historian Wallace Notestein in his *The Scot in History* writes:

> Scottish closeness or stinginess has been the quality of
> the Scots that the average man thinks of first. It seems
> to me one of the most recently observed characteristics.
> I can find hardly an allusion to Scottish closeness with
> money before the late eighteenth century.

Notestein goes on to suggest that while the English created the idea of the stingy Scot the Scots adopted this image with some pleasure.

Indeed it is very clear that the Scots, rather than resenting these reflections upon their innate generosity, have seized upon thrift as one of the distinguishing features of the race and elevated it to a morally desirable trait. Allied to thrift is the idea of poverty, which also has been promoted as a sort of moral imperative. The trade-off between poverty and sanctity was made explicit by the seventeenth century divine who wrote:

> Our neighbour nation will say of us, poor Scotland!
> beggarly Scotland! scabbed Scotland! Lousy Scotland!
> yea, but Covenanted Scotland! that makes amends
> for all.

In the twentieth century John Buchan wrote:

> Poverty is the first and biggest fact in our history, and
> from that poverty the Scottish race learned certain
> qualities that only come from a hard school. It learned
> that nothing comes without effort, and that we value
> most what costs us most.

The poverty of Scotland had, of course, been one of the points made in the Declaration of Arbroath in 1320 when the Pope was asked to:

> . . . admonish and exhort the King of England (who
> should rest content with what he has seeing that it was

enough to satisfy at least seven kings), urging him to
leave us in peace in our poor Scotland, where we live
on the uttermost bounds of human habitation and
covet nothing but our own.

This notion of Scottish poverty and thrift (if not of
actual meanness) has been exported world-wide and
appears in colloquial use in many countries. The
Germans use "Schottenpreis" – Scottish price – to
indicate rock bottom price, a bargain, and German
dictionaries record "der Schottenwitz" as "Scottish joke,
concerning thriftiness"

The Scotch obsession with money, which is not the
same things as meanness, is indeed complex. There is a
pride in poverty itself, with poverty being seen as a
morally desirable, morally superior state, a view that
sees wealth as actually or potentially corrupting. There
is also, as a concomitant to the Scottish belief in thrift,
a Scottish belief in the virtues of saving and, as a natural
development of this, an obsession with the importance
of Scottish financial institutions. These two elements in
the national psyche may for our purposes be conveniently characterised as the "Cotter's Saturday Night"
and the "Charlotte Square" obsessions.

Burns describes the family gathering in the Cotter's
simple home:

From Scenes like these, old SCOTIA's grandeur springs. . .

and goes on to pray:

Long may thy hardy sons of *rustic toil*
Be blest with health and peace and sweet content!
And O may Heaven their simple lives prevent
From *Luxury's* contagion, weak and vile!

In *A Man's a Man For A' That* Burns gives the classic form
to the Scottish assertion of the moral superiority of
honest poverty:

Is there for honest poverty
That hing's his head and a' that?
The coward slave, we pass him by -
We dare be poor for a' that!

The honest man, tho' e'r sae poor,
Is king o' men for a' that.

It is, of course, only a short step from the praise of "honest poverty" to the praise of poverty *per se* – a step which many Scots writers have taken.

It has become a conventional wisdom to describe Scotland as a poor nation, although some of the examples of conspicuous consumption indulged in by Scottish kings would surely suggest that there needs to be some qualification of this description. James IV's building of the *Great Michael*, a huge warship coveted by both Henry VIII of England and Louis XII of France, and James V's construction of an elaborate renaissance palace in Stirling Castle are hardly evidence for:

poor Scotland! beggarly Scotland! scabbed Scotland!

and it may be that Scotland's poverty was always comparative rather than absolute and that the looming presence of a large, successful and highly centralised and prosperous state to the south coloured views.

The conventional phrase "poor but honest" with its implication of honesty *despite* poverty has never found very deep roots in the Scottish mind. In fact the alternative concept of honesty *because* of poverty is much closer to the Scottish spirit. Burns's prayer in the *Cotter's Saturday Night* is :

And O may Heaven their simple lives prevent
From *Luxury's* contagion, weak and vile!
Then howe'r *crowns* and *coronets* be rent,
A *virtuous Populace* may rise the while,
And stand a wall of fire, around their much-lov'd ISLE.

Whether or not Scotland was, objectively, a poor nation or not, there seems little doubt that for much of her history she was a nation in which coinage, currency, was scarce and many payments were made in kind. Elizabeth Mure, writing of her early life on a family estate on the Renfrewshire/Ayrshire border in the first half of the eighteenth century, commented:

> Before the union, and for many years after it, money
> was very scarce in Scotland. A country without Trade,
> without Cultivation, or money to carrie on either of
> them, must improve by very slow degrees. A great part
> of the gentlemen's rents were payd in kind. This made
> them live comfortably at home, tho they could not any
> where ellse.

At the end of the eighteenth century the Minister of the parish of Luss on Loch Lomondside recorded his stipend in the *Statistical Account* in the following terms:

> The living consists of 72 bolls of oat-meal, at the rate of
> 8½ stones per boll, 6 bolls of bear, £19 12s 9d Sterling in
> money, and a good glebe.

In the next century the Perthshire estates of MacNab of MacNab were being sold and it was stated that of the £1300 rental income due each year to the estate no less than £500 was received in kind – in crops and livestock. Indeed the cattle trade of the Highlands was almost the only input of currency into those parts and the drovers performed many of the functions of a banker. Scotland was thus far from being a cash economy and this may go some way to explaining the national pre-occupation with money and the seeming glorification of poverty.

Of course this attitude to poverty made fruitful ground for humour of the Harry Lauder "bang goes saxpence" type. Lauder played up the mean Scotsman image and is quoted as saying:

If folk think I'm mean, they'll no expect too much.

A slightly subtler version of the "canny Scot" joke (and the more attractive perhaps because it is told to and about an internal audience rather than as part of a Scottish music-hall myth) is the story of the Highland exile in Glasgow summoned home to the bedside of his dying father.

> "Dugald," whispered the parent, "Luckie Simpson owes me five shullins."
>
> "Ay, man, ay," said the son eagerly.
>
> "An' Dougal More owes me seven shullins."
>
> "Ay," assented the son.
>
> "An Hamish McCraw owes me ten shullins."
>
> "Sensible tae the last," muttered the delighted heir.
>
> "Sensible to the last."
>
> "An' Dugald, I owe Calum Beg twa pounds."
>
> Dugald shook his head sadly.
>
> "Wanderin' again, wanderin' again," he sighed. "It's a peety."

This tale of lending and borrowing conveniently brings us on the Charlotte Square aspect of the Scotch obsession with money. The financial establishment of Edinburgh, centred on Charlotte Square until the demands of computer cabling and information technology drove it from those elegant Adam terraces, forms a significant counter-weight in UK terms to the City of London. It is an article of Scottish faith that our financial institutions, even those like the Bank of Scotland which were founded by Englishmen, demonstrate the innate Scottish gift for wise and prudent management of money, and display peculiarly Scottish qualities of integrity, probity and honour. Quite how this view squares with the series of ruinous bank crashes in the nineteenth century or the disaster of the Darien Scheme is, of course, a point beneath the notice of a true Scotch obsessive.

Among the talismanic idols of the Scot is the note issuing powers of the Scottish banks. This has been a dearly held privilege and one which through the years has aroused much controversy and public debate. One of the main protagonists in this battle-field was Walter Scott, who, in 1826, when London proposed to abolish the Scottish banks' privileges, responded with a series of letters, written under the pseudonym of Malachi Malagrowther. These letters are generally credited with having been highly influential in the successful campaign to retain these powers. The currency question became a focus of the campaign to maintain a distinctively Scottish identity within the Union. Scott wrote:

> We ought not to be surprised that English statesmen, and Englishmen in general, are not altogether aware of the extent of the Scottish privileges, or that they do not remember, with the same accuracy as ourselves, that we have a system of laws peculiar to us, secured by treaties.

It was over this issue that Sir Walter observed:

> If you unscotch us, you will find us damned mischievous Englishmen.

It might be thought that the question of bank-notes as a symbol of national identity is merely a historical curiosity. Such a view is refuted by the controversy which arose when the Bank of Scotland and the Clydesdale Bank followed the Bank of England's line in ceasing to print one pound notes, leaving the Royal Bank of Scotland as the only Scottish note-issuer to produce this denomination. Equally productive of regular press controversy is the degree of difficulty Scots experience in changing Scottish currency in the *bureaux de change* of Basle, Biarritz and Buddleigh Salterton.

The Scottish reputation for financial shrewdness has long been almost as much of an international cliché as the skilful Scots engineer. The rise of Andrew Carnegie from penniless mill-boy to multi-millionaire and the greatest philanthropist the world had seen can be viewed as an extreme example of an innate Scottish talent, although Carnegie's best-known apophthegm:

The man who dies thus rich, dies disgraced

suggests that Carnegie retained some of his other Scottish inheritance, a distrust of wealth and a respect for the virtues of poverty.

The evidence for the shrewd Scot is, of course, strong. One need only look at the rise of Scottish mercantile houses such as Jardine Matheson in the Far East to see the proof of this, or examine the rise of the Forbes financial empire in the United States, the foundation of an Aberdeenshire emigrant. The financing of many apparently non-Scottish enterprises proves, on closer examination, to reveal the significant presence of Scottish investors. The Cunard shipping company may have been the creation of the Canadian, Samuel Cunard, but the company would never have come into being in 1840 had not Robert Napier, the Glasgow engineer, mobilised his friends and acquaintances among the Glasgow commercial community and raised the funds for flotation. The story of railway construction in Canada is largely the story of Scottish investors and entrepreneurs.

The same type of story is told, on a more modest scale, in the history of the Savings Bank movement, whose origins are to be found in the pioneering efforts of the Rev. Henry Duncan, minister of Ruthwell in Dumfriesshire, who established in 1810 the first example of what was to become a world-wide movement. The contemporary world of investment management and insurance reveals a large share of the UK's funds and policies being managed from Scottish addresses.

The canny Scot, the close-fisted Scot, the prudent Scot, the grasping Scot. All these are indeed part of the picture, but part only. The Scots themselves cannot seem to make up their minds between the "is there for honest poverty" boast of the *Cotter's Saturday Night* aspect of the equation and the well-earned rewards of Charlotte Square. John Buchan, who wrote with such feeling about poverty as a national influence, also wrote about wealth. His retired grocer, Dickson McCunn, the hero of *Huntingtower*, is being described by his banker:

> The strength of this city. . .does not lies in its dozen very rich men, but in the hundred or two homely folk who make no parade of wealth. Men like Dickson McCunn, for example, who live all their life in a semi-detached villa and die worth half a million.

Buchan himself hardly despised the riches of this world and set most of his books in an environment of wealth and privilege although his heroes are always ready to surrender their lives of ease and comfort in a good cause.

Perhaps the best summation of the Scottish approach to money is found in neither the legends of Aberdonian miserliness or the manipulations of Charlotte Square investment analysts but in the balanced view of Burns's song, which suggests that money is important but not all important and that other values are more important:

> Contented wi' little and cantie wi' mair,
> Whene'r I foregather wi' Sorrow and Care,
> I gie them a skelp, as they're creeping alang,
> Wi' a cog o' gude swats and an auld Scottish sang.
>
> I whyles claw the elbow o' troublesome thought;
> But Man is a soger, and Life is a faught:
> My mirth and gude humour are coin in my pouch,
> And my FREEDOM's my Lairdship nae monarch dare touch.

A PECULIAR PEOPLE

The Scots and Religion

> But ye are a chosen generation, a royal priesthood,
> an holy nation, a peculiar people. . .

So runs part of the second chapter of the First Epistle of St Peter, addressed to the Christian communities in Asia Minor, but the words have often seemed to have been self applied to the Scots. In a similar way the Scots have seen themselves, in words most commonly applied to the Jews, as "a people of the Book". Religion has been a dominant and shaping influence in most societies but in Scotland a widespread and all-pervading preoccupation with religion, which can fairly be claimed to amount to obsessive proportions, has been observable at various points in the nation's history – a preoccupation which has been balanced by periods of quiescence or indifference. For example, between the passionate commitment of the Covenanting period and the equally passionate involvement of the Disruption came the long years of Moderate influence within the Church of Scotland – an era when enthusiasm was suspect and an easy middle way prevailed. However, even then, there were movements of determined and convinced dissenters prepared to divide on what now, perhaps, seem inconsequential points of doctrinal dispute – the "Lifters" and "Anti-Lifters" of the eighteenth-century, who divided on the question of the elevation of the Communion bread and wine, being an excellent example.

The individuality of Scottish religion and religious practice is, however, of much earlier origins than the Presbyterian schisms of the eighteenth century with their Auld Licht Anti- Burghers and Original Secessions. Celtic Christianity, as established in Scotland by St Columba, evolved in many ways distinct from the general pattern of Western, Roman Christianity. A more complex structure, which emphasised the role of monastic life, was one distinguishing feature; others, less profound but perhaps more evident were distinctions in the shape of the clerical tonsure or shaven head and in the date of Easter observance. As frequently happens, matters of no great significance in themselves became major symbolic issues and religion and politics became intertwined. Celtic practice had spread into north-east England with the foundation of the great Abbey at Lindisfarne as a daughter-house of Iona. The conflicting practices within his realm led the Anglian King, Oswiu, to arrange a church conference at Whitby in 664 to settle these matters. Like many such meetings since, some of those attending could not accept the decision, which favoured the Roman practice, and went off unappeased and unconvinced.

The peculiarities of Scottish religious life continued until the advent of a thoroughly obsessive religious reformer – Margaret, the Queen of Malcolm III, Malcolm Canmore. Margaret came to Scotland with a wide European experience and a commitment to mainstream Christian observance; she found in her new realm a curious mixture. There were surviving pockets of Celtic rites – the monastic settlements of the Culdees whose piety won the support of the Queen and there were also unacceptable practices which the Queen's reforms were designed to remedy.

Margaret's passion for religion was inherited by her son, David I, who became a great builder and endower of churches and monasteries, a generosity not over much appreciated by a later King, James I, who described his predecessor as:

a sair sanct for the croun

and would clearly have preferred the royal wealth to have been handed down more intact rather than being dissipated on church buildings and the endowment of masses for the repose of David's soul.

But all nations have had religious reformers and generous royal endowments – how does Scotland differ? How more religiously enthusiastic, or obsessed, are (or were) the Scots? Earlier reference was made to the sense of Scotland being a special nation, called by God. In the Declaration of Arbroath of 1320 we can find this claim being clearly enunciated, albeit in a political context – the assertion of independence from England.

This kingdom hath been governed by an uninterrupted succession of 113 kings, all of our native and royal stock, without the intervening of any stranger.

The true nobility and merits of these princes and people are very remarkable, from this one consideration (though there were no other evidence for it) that the King of Kings, the Lord Jesus Christ, after his Passion and Resurrection, honoured them as it were the first (though living in the outmost ends of the earth) with a call to His most Holy Faith: Neither would our Saviours have them confirmed in the Christian Faith by any other instrument than His own first Apostle. . . St Andrew, the most worthy brother of the Blessed Peter, whom He would always have to be over us, as our patron or protector.

This argument for the early and special calling of the Scottish people and a comparison, later in the same document, of Robert the Bruce to the Jewish heroes Joshua and Maccabeus, was designed to emphasise the distinctiveness of Scotland and the Scots – a view which few Scots in any generation have had much difficulty identifying with, however such concepts may had played in London or Rome.

The Reformation provides an excellent range of examples of Scottish religious obsessiveness and, equally, the pre-Reformation period provides an example of a period of comparative religious quiescence and decline, although the process of internal reform had started to take shape before the continental ideas of Luther and Calvin arrived.

George Wishart's burning for heresy, under the gaze of Cardinal David Beaton at St Andrews in March 1546 is echoed by the slaying of the Cardinal two months later – a divine judgement in the opinion of the not un-obsessive John Knox:

> James Melven. . . said, "This work and judgement
> of God ought to be done with greater gravity," and
> presenting unto him the point of the sweard, said,
> "Repent thee of thy former wicked life, but especially
> of the schedding of the blood of that noble instrument
> of God, Maister George Wishart. . ." And so he stroke
> him twice or thrice through with a stog sweard.

A century later, in the signing of the National Covenant, a popularly and widely supported statement of the claims of the reformed church against the feared encroachments of Charles I's Anglicanism, we see again both the extent of religious enthusiasm in Scotland and the sense of a special destiny. Not only was the Covenant document signed by a large number of nobles, gentry, ministers and representatives of the

Royal Burghs, but the whole exercise was seen, in a contemporary phrase, as:

> . . . the glorious marriage day of the Kingdom with God

When, four years later, the Civil War broke out and the Scots allied themselves with the English Parliamentarians, the distinctiveness of a Scots approach was noted. In the words of the Rev. Robert Baillie, a leading figure in the Covenanting party:

> The English were for a civil League; we for a
> religious Covenant

and had the Scots had their way they would have imposed Scottish style Presbyterianism on England and the English as the price for their military assistance in the South.

After Charles II's Restoration the struggle for religious supremacy broke out afresh. Events such as the Pentland Rising of 1666 and the Covenanting Rising of 1679 with its battles at Drumclog and Bothwell Bridge proving both the potency of religious ideas among Scots of all classes and their tendency to take debate on these matters to an extreme and to invite martyrdom and welcome death. The dying words of Hugh McKail, captured and tortured after the Pentland Rising, well illustrate this tendency:

> Farewell, sun, moon and stars. Farewell, kindred and
> friends, farewell, world and time, farewell, weak and frail
> body. Welcome eternity, welcome angels and saints.

The period of the later Covenanting movement displays an intolerance and violence on both sides which does little credit to Christianity, with the Government forces torturing and killing and the Covenant extremists murdering Archbishop Sharp in front of his daughter. Although the number of deaths in the "Killing Times" were scarcely as high as folklore and Protestant hagiography would suggest (the seventeenth-century had much to learn from our own age about butchery and oppression), there nonetheless was, in some areas at least, a widespread and principled popularly based struggle for a preferred form of worship and church government. Severe legislation was enacted against the Covenanters:

> whosoever without licence or authoritie shall preach, expound scripture or pray at any of these meetings in the feild. . . or who shall convocat any number of people to these meetings shall be punished with death and confiscation of their goods. (Act of 1670).

The more extreme faction, under Richard Cameron – the Cameronians – took their concern for church government to the extent, in 1680, of repudiating their allegiance to Charles II, whom they characterised as a tyrant, usurper and enemy to Christ:

> . . . we for ourselves and all that will adhere to us, as the representative of the true presbyterian kirk and covenanted nation of Scotland. . . do by thir presents disown Charles Stuart, that has been reigning (or rather tyrannizing as we may say) on the throne of Britain these years bygone. . .

A more acceptable form of religious passion and struggle was to be seen in the Disruption of 1843. The Established Church of Scotland had become deeply divided on various issues but the critical point of separation was on the right of congregations to make a free choice of their ministers as opposed to having a pastor presented to the parish by a lay patron. Those in the Kirk who could no longer accept this position left the 1843 General Assembly and established the Free Church of Scotland. For the man and woman in the pew this was a solemn step, to leave the church of their fathers, but around a third of the communicant members of the Auld Kirk did so. For the 474 ministers who established the Free Church it meant a great deal more – it was the loss of status, as part of the official structure of society; it was the loss of a secure income; it was the loss of their church building and it was the loss of their home. The clergy and people who left the Established Church in the rational and scientific mid-nineteenth-century were, in their way, just as convinced, just as unyielding, just as obsessed, as the Cameronians of the seventeenth century. With energy and conviction they set about duplicating the religious and educational and social provision of the Auld Kirk, and in a few years had done so almost totally, though not without local difficulties as the judge, Lord Cockburn, noted:

> In some places, where whole parishes are the property of one man, and he a tyrant, the people, denied a spot of ground even to stand upon, and not allowed to obstruct the high road, have been obliged to assemble for the worship of God in the way that their consciences approve of on the sea-shore, between low ands high water-mark.

But, it may be argued, that was the nineteenth century, still an age of faith. What evidence is there for a continuing Scotch obsession with religion at the end of the twentieth century? At first one might think that there is little. One of the characteristics of Scottish religiosity was an extreme Sabbatarianism, of the type revealed in the story of the Englishman visiting the Highlands who took a walk on the Sunday afternoon. Reproved for this breach of the Sabbath the Englishman ventured to suggest:

> Did not our Lord walk in the fields with his apostles on the Sabbath day?

to which the unyielding elder of the Kirk replied:

Aye, but we think nae mair of Him here for that.

Many of the evidences of religion, such as Sabbath observance, have now all but vanished in Scotland – more so even than in England. It was Scotland, after all which was first to have her supermarkets, garden centres, and those modern temples to domestic improvement, the DIY Centres, open on Sundays. True, the ferries still do not run to some of the Western Isles on Sundays and members of some of the more rigorous sects will not countenance the purchase of a Sunday paper, printed on Saturday (curiously the purchase of a newspaper on Monday, despite the fact that it was printed on Sunday, seems not to cause them the same theological difficulties). But in general the more obvious and bizarre manifestations of Sabbath observance have gone – in living memory children's swings in parks were chained up on a Sunday and no respectable tenement dweller would have hung out washing to dry on a Sunday.

It might be argued that the denominational rivalries which still afflict, in particular, West Central Scotland and which have their obvious, and unlovely, manifestations in Rangers and Celtic football clubs and in accusations of denominational favouritism in local government, are evidence of religious obsession. Certainly the devotees of Ibrox and Parkhead are obsessed but few on the Ibrox terracing would be found sound if examined on the Shorter Catechism or the Westminster Confession of Faith, and few on the Parkhead terracing are likely to be able to give a coherent account of the Roman Catholic teaching on transubstantiation or explain the development of priestly celibacy with particular reference to the edicts of Pope Leo the Great. These obsessives, and their fellow-travellers in Orange Orders and Hibernian Societies, are less an example of religious obsession than of acute and unreconstructed tribalism. If a deeply rooted concern with religion is still a Scottish characteristic, then evidence needs to be sought elsewhere.

The Church of Scotland, though reduced in numbers, still has over three quarters of a million members and 1,700 churches – the latter number admittedly a legacy of the enthusiastic and schismatic tendency of earlier centuries. For all that the Kirk is now a minority interest, it is significant that its annual General Assembly still commands surprisingly substantial press, radio and television coverage. Quite why this gathering attracts more coverage than a political party conference or a trade union conference is debatable. It may not entirely be due to Scottish religious enthusiasm – to an extent it is certainly a reflection of the General Assembly's role as a surrogate parliament for a stateless nation. However, even this quasi-political function surely raises the question of why, in an allegedly secular age, the annual convention of a religious denomination, even one that is "the Church by law established", has the authority to discharge such a role. Perhaps it is simply custom and practice and nobody has yet felt it apt to comment that the Emperor is without clothes. However, an instructive comparison can be made betweeen the coverage given to the Kirk's General Assembly and that devoted to the Church of England's General Synod – a broadly similar body whose deliberations command little attention unless proposals on the ordination of women or the status of homosexuals are on the agenda.

There remain other indications that what Walter Scott called:

> . . . a strong Scotch accent of the mind. . .

still has as one of its essential components a religious inclination. One might cite the remarkable success of William Lorrimer's translation of the New Testament into Scots, tentatively published in hardback in 1983 but swiftly achieving the mass-market distinction of a Penguin paperback edition in 1985. One might equally well cite the newspaper headlines following Margaret Thatcher's speech to the General Assembly in 1988, which picking up the fact that the Assembly Hall is on Edinburgh's Mound, characterised the Prime Ministerial address as "The Sermon on the Mound", surely relying on at least a nodding acquaintance with Matthew's Gospel among their readers.

The evidence of statistics is clear – Scotland retains a significantly higher level of church membership than does England. To take the two established Churches, the Church of Scotland has 770,000 communicant members; an exactly equivalent figure does not seem to exist for the Church of England, but authoritative sources speak of around 1.2 million attending services each Sunday. Admittedly these figures are not comparable, but even allowing for only a percentage of Kirk members actually darkening the doors of their parish church each Sunday it is hard, remembering the 10:1 population ratio, to avoid the conclusion that Scotland remains, if not a more religious, at least a more church-going and church-conscious nation than its southern neighbour.

Were further evidence sought one might do worse than look to the immense popularity of the lugubrious television clergyman, the Rev. I.M. Jolly, created by the Scots actor, Ricky Fulton, and regularly, indeed religiously, presented on television at New Year. The popularity of this caricature of a dismal, kill-joy, Scottish clergyman, which, like all caricatures and clichés, demands a certain awareness of the terms of reference for maximum effect, suggests that there still remains something of a shared religious culture at large in late twentieth century Scotland.

A SCOTSMAN ON THE MAKE

The Scots Abroad

From the lone shieling of the misty island
Mountains divide us, and the waste of seas -
Yet still the blood is strong, the heart is Highland,
And we in dreams behold the Hebrides.

There is surely a rich vein of irony in Scotland producing so much literature on the theme of a nostalgic longing for home, works like the *Canadian Boat Song* quoted above, while being, with the possible exception of the Jews, the most successfully scattered and far travelled of the world's races. What has distinguished the Scot as a traveller is not simply the extent of his travels, for others have travelled as far; nor the number of Scots who travelled, for other countries have arguably sent just as large a proportion of their people overseas; but the enthusiasm with which Scots have left "the lone shieling" and the mill terrace, the miner's row and the ancestral mansion to seek freedom, fame, fortune and fulfilment in the uttermost parts of the earth. Well could J. M. Barrie write in *What Every Woman Knows*:

My lady, there are few more impressive sights in
the world than a Scotsman on the make.

The impressive adaptability of the Scot to life "furth of Scotland" is attested to by the lives of French bishops, Russian admirals, Indian Nabobs and German Field Marshals who had but two things in common – their Scottishness and their ambition.

The Auld Alliance is perhaps the most formal and most famous example of this Scottish interconnection with foreign lands. Most treaties and alliances are simply mechanisms between governments entered into for reasons of state – and the Auld Alliance was certainly that. However in its 265 years of active life, between the Treaty of Paris in 1295 and the Treaty of Edinburgh of 1560, it became part of the fabric of Scottish life and its influences are still to be seen. It is unlikely that such a political treaty would have been so influential had not there been an underlying propensity for foreign travel, trade and settlement among the Scottish people.

The connection with France operated on a variety of different levels. Scholars, like Duns Scotus and George Buchanan, travelled to Paris and the other French universities to study and to teach. Scots merchants sent ships to Bordeaux to bring home the red wine that was indeed the other national drink. Armies were sent to France to fight against England. Scots were likely to turn up everywhere and anywhere – when Joan of Arc relieved Orleans in 1429 her troops entered the city led by a banner painted by a Scotsman and were greeted by the Bishop of Orleans – John de Kirkmichael, a Scot, probably hailing from Douglasdale in Lanarkshire. The Scottish army which had gone to France to fight for the Dauphin was led by John Stuart of Darnley, who was rewarded with the Lordship of Aubigny-sur-Nère, and the Stuarts of Aubigny became generals of the French army, commanders of the bodyguard of the French kings, and exemplified the "Auld Alliance". To this day the quiet little town of Aubigny, in the Department of

Cher, still proclaims itself as the "Cité des Stuarts" and the chateau of the Stuarts now houses a museum dedicated to the "Vieille Alliance Franco-Ecossaise".

France was perhaps an obvious country for Scots to move to, to travel in, to trade with, if only on the age-old principle of an enemy's enemy being your friend. But even after the excuse of a mutual suspicion of England had passed into history, the Scots fascination with France continued. John Law, the son of an Edinburgh goldsmith, established an amazing ascendancy over the French government in early eighteenth-century and was responsible for the establishment of the Bank of France, for the French development of the Mississippi area and ended up as Comptroller General of France – before all his schemes ended in ruin and bankruptcy. However Law was just one of many Scots who displayed an affinity with France and an identification with her. At the end of the nineteenth-century Robert Louis Stevenson was another; his step-son Lloyd Osbourne wrote:

> France had a profound influence over Stevenson;
> mentally he was half a Frenchman; in tastes, habits
> and prepossessions he was almost wholly French. . . he
> loved both country and people, and was more really at
> home in France than anywhere else.

France had for Scots, from Duns Scotus to Stevenson, the charm of foreignness coupled with reasonable proximity and something of a shared culture. Russia seems to offer much less with its remoteness and alien ways. Yet Russia, or in earlier years, Muscovy, attracted a bewildering number and variety of Scots who saw in the Tsar's wide domains opportunities for advancement – but more than simple ambition would seem to have been at work here.

A Russian academic, Dimitry Federov, has written of this Scotch invasion:

There were some notable Anglo-Russian families, but
on the whole the English tended to serve *in* Russia not
for her, whereas the Scots appeared much more willing
and successful in settling down permanently among
the alien, even hostile, environment.

This perception, which could be echoed from many of
the other centres of the Scottish Diaspora, suggests
something of the Scots success in their relations with
foreign lands – a capacity to identify with the host
community. Such identification did not, of course,
mean a merging of identity – the string of Caledonian
Societies, Burns Clubs and St Andrews Societies around
the globe testify to the portable nature of Scotland but
there is a very clear sense in which the Scots seem to
have found it easy to adjust to even the most alien of
societies. The Russian case provides many examples.
General Tam Dalyell of the Binns entered the Tsar's
service in 1655, remaining there for ten years before
returning to Scotland, bringing with him much
experience of war and that useful instrument of torture,
the thumb-screws, all of which he was to put to use in
the suppression of the Covenanters. Bishop Burnet
wrote:

> Dalyell acted the Muscovite too grossly. He threatened
> to spit men and to roast them.

In naval matters as well as in military ones the Scots
were to the fore in Russia, with a remarkable number
rising to become Admirals in the Russian service. Quite
how dominant the Scots were in the Russian forces is
demonstrated by a quotation from the *Scots Magazine*
of 1739:

> At the head of the Russian fleet we find a Gordon, in the
> highest rank of the army a Keith, and Douglas, Lesley;
> and many more. . .

Perhaps most notable of these naval Scots was Samuel Greig, a native of Inverkeithing, who rose to the rank of Admiral and developed the great naval base at Kronstadt in the 1780s.

More peaceful contacts with Russia are demonstrated by the proprietors of pre-revolutionary Moscow's largest department store, Messrs Muir and Mirrielees, and by the architects, doctors and engineers who were attracted there. One of the most striking examples of this movement came in the 1784 when Charles Cameron was appointed as architect to Catherine the Great and advertised in the *Edinburgh Evening Courant* for clerks of works, master masons, master bricklayers, a master smith, journeymen plasterers and journeymen bricklayers. In all seventy-three workers signed up for the enterprise and they and as many wives and children left Scotland for St Petersburg. Such movements were not unprecedented – ten years earlier a group of workmen from the Carron Ironworks near Falkirk had gone out to Kronstadt to install a steam-powered water pump. For a nation which has often been accused of a parochial preoccupation with its own kailyard, this willingness, on the part of artisans and craftsmen, to travel to what must have been almost unimaginably remote and alien lands is surely noteworthy.

Not all Scots abroad were admirals or generals or architects. The Scottish merchant was a familiar figure all around northern Europe. Some of these were in a very small way of business – pedlars or packmen. Sir John Skene, writing in the sixteenth-century, noted that these pedlars were to be found in:

> . . .ane great multitude in the town of Cracovia,
> ann. Dom. 1569.

and doubtless in other towns in Poland and the Baltic states the Scottish merchant was a regular visitor. On a larger scale, the Scottish trade with the Low Countries had long been conducted through a Scottish Staple Port. The origins of this trading station, originally at Middleburg, certainly date back to the fourteenth-century. Later the port moved to Bruges and finally was located at Campvere on the Dutch island of Walcheren. Here a "Conservator of Scots privileges" had his seat and attempted to regulate transactions between Scots merchants and the host community. The main commodities traded by these Scots merchants were linen and woollen cloth and salt, and for obvious geographical reasons most of this trade with Scandinavia, the Hanseatic League states around the Baltic and the Low Countries was carried out from Scotland's east coast ports.

French trade, particularly the wine trade with Bordeaux, was more evenly spread with many ships and merchants passing back and forward from the Clyde ports as well as from Leith and the Fife ports. The following entry from the Dumbarton Register of Ship Entries could be echoed from many of the other Royal Burghs with foreign trading privileges:

> 1595, March 12 – Johne Smollet, yunger, burgess off Dumbartane enterit his schippe callit the Providence off Dunbartane now cum into the Clyd at Newark ladyn wt. fyftie tunes hie cuntrie wynes laidnit at Bordeouss.

We perhaps tend to think of emigration in terms of the colonies or that significant ex-colony the United States of America (and the Scotch obsession with America merits a chapter to itself) but it is important to remember the many Scots who settled permanently in European countries, often becoming important figures in their new homes, and of course succeeding genera-tions became even more surely part of the host society. Atypical, perhaps, but nonetheless interesting as demonstrations of the results of the Scottish ability to move into a new society and identify with it, are the Norwegian composer Edvard Grieg, the descendant of Aberdonian Alexander Greig; Mikhail Lermontov, the Russified poet descendant of a Scots Learmont, and the Napoleon's Marshal, the Duke of Taranto, Jacques Macdonald, son of a Jacobite exile.

At the beginning of the seventeenth century Scots were prominent in the armies of the Swedish king Gustavus Adolphus and during the Thirty Years War he employed no less than thirteen regiments of Scottish infantry in his service, besides many Scots officers in other units. So ubiquitous were the Scots in the Thirty Years War that the eccentric seventeenth-century writer, Sir Thomas Urquhart, claimed it as a demonstration that the Scottish nation was unconquerable:

> . . . what battel soever, at any time these forty years past
> hath been struck within the continent of Europe, all the
> Scots that fought in that field, were never overthrown
> and totally routed; for if some of them were captives and
> taken prisoners, others of that nation were victorious,
> and givers of quarter; valour and mercy on the one side,
> with misfortune and subjection upon the other side,
> meeting one another in the persons of compatriots on
> both sides. . .

Exile, for one cause or another, was as important a motivation as ambition for the wandering Scots. The religious and political turmoil of the seventeenth-century and particularly the Civil War drove many Scots overseas, and the failure of the Jacobite cause was another reason for temporary or permanent settlement overseas. In the eighteenth-century, two of the most distinguished military and diplomatic figures in Europe were the Scots Jacobite exiles George Keith, the Earl Marischal, Ambassador for Frederick the Great to

Madrid and Paris, and his brother James who after service in the Spanish and Russian armies became a Field Marshal in the Prussian army. Another characteristically Scottish reason for travel was cultural improvement. As James Boswell wrote to Jean Jacques Rousseau:

> You were indeed right to congratulate me when my father gave me permission to travel in Italy. Nine months in this delicious country have done more for me than all the sage lessons which books, or men formed by books, could have taught me. It was my imagination that needed correction, and nothing but travel could have produced this effect.

Sometimes these two sorts of Scots abroad could meet and Boswell performed part of his Grand Tour in 1764-1766 in the company of the Earl Marischal, by this time pardoned by the British government although he never returned to his ancestral lands. This somewhat unlikely pair of travelling companions – the Jacobite Earl was 75 and Boswell, the son of a pillar of the Scottish Whig establishment, was 24 – seem to have shared many sentiments. Boswell wrote enthusiastically to Dr Johnson:

> My Lord Marischal is so good as to take me with him to Germany. . . Think only of my happiness now to travel with the ancient Scottish nobleman who has seen so much of the world in all its grandeur and all its pleasure; who is at courts as I am in the houses of Ayrshire lairds. . .

The Earl later was to demonstrate that 50 years in exile and high office in the Prussian King's service had made him no less a Scot. Boswell noted in his diary for 6th September 1764 that the Earl:

> . . . took down from his bookcase the history of Robert the Bruce in old verse, and made me a present of it,

writing upon it, "Scotus Scoto" [From one Scot to
another] and saying "Now you must read this once
every year." I had almost cried before the good
old man.

Boswell's travels in Europe had started with his being
sent to Utrecht, in Holland, to continue his legal studies.
This was a very common Scottish custom. The intellectual
roots of Scots Law were to be found in the Roman and
Dutch systems and this ancestry meant that many
Scots advocates, down to the end of the eighteenth-
century, completed their legal education at Utrecht, or
as Boswell's father and grandfather had done, at Leyden.
Boswell's Grand Tour, as we have seen, took him to Italy
– another very noted centre of Scottish travel, study and
influence. Many Scottish travellers could, like Boswell,
have apostrophised that land:

O Italy! Land of felicity! True seat of all elegant delight!

One particular form of "elegant delight" which attracted
many Scots to Italy was art. The inspiration of the
classical and renaissance artists and the practical
training of contemporary masters drew Scottish artists
from William Aikman, who studied in Rome from
1707-10, through Gavin Hamilton (who was to settle
in Rome permanently) to Allan Ramsay and Henry
Raeburn. All found their careers enhanced by the
cachet of study in Italy and their skills honed by their
experiences there.

Unlike the colonies in the Americas or the Antipodes
few Scots went to India as permanent settlers. Rather
they went – as soldiers, missionaries, administrators,
merchants, teachers, engineers, doctors – with the
idea of returning to Scotland; but they certainly went in
great quantities. It was Sir Walter Scott who wrote that
India was:

> . . . the corn chest for Scotland where we poor gentry
> must send our younger sons as we send our black
> cattle to the south.

One event which greatly facilitated this Scottish invasion of India was the rise to political power of Henry Dundas, who among his various appointments was President of the Board of Control for India, and used appointments in the Indian administration as one of his tools for exercising political control in Scotland. Scott's "poor gentry" often had their votes bought by the promise of a post for their "younger sons".

In the mid nineteenth-century the opening up of Burma to British trade and influence saw the rise of great Scottish run companies like P. Henderson & Coy. "Paddy Henderson" and its associate the Irrawaddy Flotilla Company, whose Dumbarton-built paddle steamers and Dumbarton-trained engineers sailed the rivers of the Irrawaddy Delta and whose contribution was recorded by Rudyard Kipling:

> Come you back to Mandalay,
> Where the old Flotilla lay:
> Can't you 'ear their paddles
>   chunkin' from Rangoon to Mandalay?

Many of the Scots who went to India returned with great, and, it must be confessed, sometimes dubiously obtained, wealth. These "Nabobs" as they were nick-named, were of course, only a minority of the Scots who went to India, however much they symbolised the "Scotsman on the make". Many others succumbed to the climate, devoted themselves to missionary and medical work or experienced great privations – although the story of the notoriously irascible Scottish soldier David Baird reminds us that others could suffer from the Scots. Baird had been captured by Hyder Ali, the Rajah of Mysore, and word came back to his mother that he and the other British captives were held in Seringapatam, chained together in pairs. His unsentimental mother's comment was:

> I pity the man wha's chained to oor Davie.

In civil administration, as well as in military life and commerce, the Scots were disproportionately represented in British India. Even at the highest level, the Governors General and Viceroys, the record shows a curious preponderance of Scottish names – Dalhousie, Minto, Elgin, Linlithgow, Macpherson.

The Scots may have been driven overseas by ambition, economic necessity, political pressure, a sense of adventure, a need for higher education and many other reasons. Daniel Defoe, in his *A Tour Through the Whole Island of Great Britain (1726),* wrote that Scotland could be improved by:

> A change in the disposition of the common people,
> from a desire of travelling abroad, and wandering
> from home, to an industrious and dilligent
> application to labour at home.

This does suggest that Scottish wanderlust was well established and well known and there seems little doubt that they travelled abroad in exceptionally large numbers. In consequence the concept of foreign travel and life abroad must have spread throughout the whole population. Most families would have a friend or relation who had gone overseas – a soldier with Gustavus Adolphus or a clerk with the East India Company, a student of law at Leyden or a trader in the Baltic. The influence that these contacts must have had on what we often, erroneously, think of as an inward-looking and closed society, cannot be underestimated. Neil Munro's novel *John Splendid* opens with the hero,

Colin, returning to Inveraray from service abroad. He reflects on how he had planned the manner of his home-coming:

> But it was not until I had run away from Glasgow College, and shut the boards for good and all, as I thought, on my humane letters and history, and gone with cousin Gavin to the German wars in Mackay's Corps of true Highlanders, that I added a manlier thought to my thinking of the day when I should come home to my native place. I've seen me in the camp at night, dog-wearied after stoury marching on their cursed foreign roads, keeping my eyes open and the sleep at an arm's-length, that I might think of Shira Glen.

As travellers and soldiers like Colin returned (those that did return), so the travellers' tales of strange places and strange ways would be told and re-told in croft-house and castle and new generations would absorb the Scotch obsession with foreign parts – an obsession which continued to co-exist with the exile's obsession with Scotland.

> Mountains divide us, and the waste of seas –
> Yet still the blood is strong, the heart is Highland. . .

THE TARTAN ARMY

The Scots and Sport

The distinctive Scotch obsession here is not an obsession with sport in general and for its own sake, as, to be fair, has been true of the English, the great keepers of the Corinthian spirit. Scotland's is an obsession of an intenser hue, with a smaller number of sports, each with its own distinctive social pattern of followers and participants. A democratic interest in some forms of sport and games is not exclusive to Scots – the USA's peculiar sports of baseball and football don't from this distance appear to be class specific – but there does appear to be a strong popular and more democratic character to Scottish sport.

Golf, for example, has been played by all classes in this country, in curious contrast to the symbol of wealth and privilege which it has become in every other country to which it has been transported. Robert Burns, the ploughman poet, isn't known as a golfer, nor indeed a sportsman of any sort, but in *Epistle to Davie* he seems to make reference to the common view of the game as subject to fickle fortune, almost in the manner of a clubhouse raconteur:

The honest heart that's free frae a'
Intended fraud or guile,
However Fortune kick the ba',
Has aye some cause to smile

In their origins sport and games in Scotland probably had a utilitarian function. Competing at wrestling, foot races and Scottish specialties like hurling the stone and tossing the caber (a Celtic word meaning a beam) – a perversely difficult activity which is surely due for discovery as a televised spectacle – were good for developing warriors' qualities of skill, strength and endurance. Celtic tales speak of chieftains keeping a large rock or two handy for trying the mettle of their followers or of challengers from abroad.

Right from the outset, however, there were signs that sports and games would be seen as a badge of class, rank or privilege, for there was one field sport that was largely reserved for the few, perhaps the warrior class or perhaps for the leader's immediate coterie, and that was the chase, the Royal Hunt. The splendid hunting scenes carved on Pictish and on neo-Pictish stones like the one at St Andrews Cathedral show only the few in pursuit of the quarry, with the many doubtless employed in beating and flushing out activities and, at least in the later medieval period, savagely punished for spoiling the king's sport. The chase, or pursuit of animals, first on foot, and then on horseback, was the most prized form of hunting, with other forms, like falconry, also flourishing in the Scottish countryside.

> The stag at eve had drunk his fill,
> Where danced the moon on Monan's rill,
> And deep his midnight lair had made
> In lone Glenartney's hazel shade;
> But when the sun his beacon red
> Had kindled on Benvoirlich's head,
> The deep-mouthed blood-hound's heavy bay
> Resounded up the rocky way,
> And faint, from farther distance borne,
> Were heard the clanging hoof and horn.
>   Walter Scott, *The Lady of the Lake*

The modern era has seen the disappearance of this view of hunting and the pursuit of God's creatures for sport survives only in respect of the once aristocratic and now plutocratic sport of stalking, fishing, often said to be the most popular of all sports, and, perhaps, venery's disreputable successor and *alter ego*, poaching. Neil Munro's Para Handy describes his methods:

> I have a bit o' a net there no' the size of a pocket-
> naipkin, that I use noo and then at the river-mooths.
> I chust put it doon – me and Dougie – and whiles
> a salmon or a sea-troot meets wi' an accident and
> gets into't.

His accomplice Dougie is asked why he is so carefully feeling all over a haul of six salmon and replies:

> . . . I wass frightened they might be the laird's salmon,
> and I wass lookin' for the luggage label on them.
> There's none. It's all right, they're chust wild salmon
> that nobody planted.
>   *Para Handy, Poacher*

Poaching of course is not confined to the capture of fish, but also to the illegal killing of deer and other game. The thrill of the chase, of which the huntsman speaks, can only be compared to the excitement of the contest between poacher and keeper or gillie. John Buchan brings all these simmering ingredients to the boil in the splendidly anarchic *John Macnab,* where the sportsmen turn poacher and form unholy alliances against landowners and the highest and the lowest combine against the unspeakable *nouveaux riches*.

But right from the start, golf was seen as capable of creating an obsessive interest among its followers, and one which even offered a kind of threat to the state, as was another sport, football, with great popular appeal. In 1457, James II ordered that "the fut bal and the golf be utterly cryit downe and nocht usit", just as his father, James I, had previously instructed, on his release from many years of captivity in England, that "nae man play at the football under pain of four pence". Both monarchs saw these games as evidence of frittering away of citizens' time which might have better been spent in practising the arts of archery or similar warlike pursuits of more use to the state. At the same time, though, James V, Mary, James VI and James VII are all recorded players of the game. The king might even have warned of the danger of "golf widows" being created, though not quite in the modern sense:

> For Sale: Set of golf clubs. A snip at £100. If a man
> answers the phone, hang up.
> [Small ad. in *The Sunday Post*]

This strange, cross-country pastime, which the cynic is apt to describe as "A good walk spiled", presents an interesting changing social pattern throughout its history. Beginning as sport of kings, golf then acquired the mark of a more bourgeois sport, and its followers, like the Honourable Company of Gentlemen Golfers of Edinburgh, with their links at Leith, and others at St Andrews and Prestwick, were very much kings of their ain middens, with the lower classes supposedly content to act as hewers of wood and drawers of water, or as caddies at any rate.

Then, in the later part of the nineteenth and early twentieth centuries, the game enjoyed an amazing rise in popularity, reminiscent of the railway boom, and in many parts of the country it acquired a more artizan character, which survives today, even in the face of the great wave of commercialisation of sport. It also entered into popular social and cultural consciousness as can seen by the amazing amount of artefacts and memorabilia, not to say tat, which accompanies the game today.

The so-called tented villages at the great championships like the Open display a wide range of goods, from oil paintings nearly as long as the holes they depict to whisky glasses by the hundred, and these are but the modern equivalent of the embroidered tea-cosies and samplers of former years. But here we are touching on another Scotch obsession – the production of tartanised kitsch of a particularly virulent form (*cf* C. John Taylor).

Medieval football seems to have been obsessive indeed. In 1511 the Privy Council described it as "wood" or mad football – evidence that there always has been a hooligan element. In 1607 youths in Aberdeen were had up for profaning the Sabbath by "drinking, playing football, dancing and roving from parish to parish", and even today the "town games" which survive, like the "Ba'" game in Kirkwall, are uninhibited in action and the talk of the town for days on end.

The story of modern or Association football, so-called because it followed the rules laid down in the 1860s by an association of clubs under the distinguished leadership of Oxford University, is a curious regression within a century from blazered toffs through cloth caps to bare chests and tribal chants – a case of reverting to its primitive roots perhaps? The nineteenth century did see many changes in the game, like the rise of professionalism. And as always, there were Scotsmen on the make. In 1878, a team including two professionals from Partick played in the FA Cup fourth round at the Oval against the Old Etonians!

This was also the heyday of the villages and small towns, when the likes of Renton and Dumbarton might share a championship with Glasgow Rangers or Preston North End.

Tonight the conqueror's banner in Renton town's unfurled
To welcome home their heroes, the champions of the
world;

The band in triumph playing – the busy stir's began
And the fire of victory's blazing on the braes of old
    Carman.

For we, as honest Scotchmen, should honour and admire
The hardy lads we've reared and trained in old
    Dumbartonshire;
And when you meet the Preston team, be careful how
    you play,
And beat them, as you played and beat your Southern
    foes to-day.

As has been said, the Scots footballers were among the first to sally forth as mercenaries. Neil Munro's story in *Erchie, My Droll Friend*, gives a curiously modern account of a transfer, involving the vast sum of £4,500 in the 1920s.

Tom Hamilton doesna' handle a' that money; it maistly gangs to the Kilmarnock club that sold him. A' he gets frae the Preston North End is his wages and expenses. Bein' a champion fitba player's no great catch; he's the last relic o' slavery left in modern times. He has nae sooner settled doon in a nice wee hoose wi' a bit o' gairden than somebody comes and buys him and cairts him awa' to anither pairt o' the country where he doesna ken a livin' soul and has to learn the language.

    The Footballer's Life

The growth of the professional game in the twentieth-century led to the mass participation in a weekly ritual – something which gave shape and meaning to working class lives. Hundreds of thousands of people were involved in almost medieval pilgrimages. Great cathedrals of the game like Hampden and Ibrox were the biggest stadia in the world at the time.

He was among enthusiasts of his own persuasion. In consonance with ancient custom the police had

shepherded supporters of the Rangers to one end of the
ground and supporters of the Celtic to the other: so far
as segregation was possible with such a great mob of
human beings. . . For nearly two hours thereafter
Danny Shields lived far beyond himself in a whirling
world of passion. . . in delight in the cunning moves of
[the players], in their tricks and asperities, the men on
the terraces found release from the drabness of their
own industrial degradation.

   George Blake, *The Shipbuilders*

But then with the war, there was a dawning recognition
that the days of world leadership had gone. New names
like Moscow Dynamo and Inter Milan formed part of
conversations in pub and factory, along with a growing
respect. A brief flourish came in 1967, when Celtic won
the European Cup and created legends of the "lost
legions" who never returned from Lisbon, but already
many a Scots football supporter was turning into a couch
potato. And those who remained on the terracings were
taking refuge in a kind of self-conscious romanticism
not unlike the nineteenth century.

   Walter Scott had been an early promoter of the game
and its all-round effectiveness. In 1815 he sponsored a
grand match between Selkirk and Yarrow in Ettrick
Forest:

Then strip lads and to it, though sharp be the weather
And if by mischance you should happen to fall
There are worse things in life than a tumble on heather
And life is itself but a game of football

and he would have recognised the characteristics of the
phase into which football now moved.

   This was the era of the "Tartan Army". Looking and
behaving like a meeting of the Sealed Knot Society,
the supporters of the national team took on a sort of

historical re-enactment of battles from Scotland's past. In particular, there was a curious echo of the last great military campaign on British soil, with the tartan-clad hordes in the place of the Jacobites of the '45 Rebellion and the matches of the 1978 Argentina World Cup as a symbolic rendering of the battles of that doomed army. For was not football a splendid example of the Celts' affinity for relishing lost causes and even defeats? And goodness knows we had plenty practice! For the Tartan Army had a Young Pretender in Ally Macleod, the national manager and Argentina was his Culloden, with the part of Cumberland's dragoons taken by other Scots, led by the traitorous `fans with typewriters' of the press, who turned on their former heroes.

This, then, is something of the Scots obsession for sport. Much could be said about other games which have caught the imagination of groups, or even of many. Of bowling, with its distinctive class structure, but a sport in which the Scots gave the world its distinctive form, by writing down the "laws" and defining the code in the ways that the English did for cricket. Or of shinty, which is played with passionate intensity and controlled violence which might have attracted an Ossian. Or rugby, which only in the Borders has managed to shake off its elitist overtones, yet currently shares with soccer a new "anthem" which combines bad grammar with shaky history.

Finally, though, it has often been remarked that it is football, "wud football", which is a kind of symbol of at least one face of the nation, and we are reminded of Bill Shankly's definitive summing up, when being told that football was a matter of life or death. Shankly's rejoinder was, "It's more serious than that!"

McAndrew's Hymn

The Scots and Technology

From coupler-flange to spindle-guide I see Thy Hand,
   O God –
Predestination in the stride o' yon connectin'-rod.
John Calvin might ha' forged the same – enormous,
   certain, slow –
Ay, wrought it in the furnace-flame – my 'Institutio'.

When Rudyard Kipling had a ship's engineer muse on predestination, grace, sin and technology the Anglo-Indian poet inevitably, and we might think almost automatically, made the engineer a Clydeside Scot. When the American writer Gene Roddenberry created his immensely successful television series *Star Trek,* the starship *Enterprise's* chief engineer was equally inevitably named Scotty. (The filling of the role by James Doohan, an Irish-American actor, with a less than convincing Scottish accent, reflects more on the casting consultant and the vagaries of the mass media than on the argument of this chapter.)

What Kipling and Roddenberry shared was a simple but profound conviction that the Scots were synonymous with engineering and technology, whether the technology of the triple expansion steam engine or the technology of the warp drive and the photon torpedo.

This conviction is, of course, enthusiastically shared by the Scots themselves – and with some justification. The Scottish role in the Industrial Revolution was a disproportionately significant one, the shipbuilding and engineering impact of the River Clyde was immense, the civil engineering skills of Scots shaped much of the modern world. Some measure of Scottish scientific and technological genius is given by the intriguing fact that Scotland (population 5 million) has won more Nobel prizes than Japan (population 123 million).

Scotland's scientific reputation would seem to date from the second half of the eighteenth-century, although there are high points from earlier centuries. High points (both literal and metaphorical); consider the case of the Brother Damian, the Friar of Tungland and his aeronautical experiments at Stirling Castle in 1508. John Lesley, a Scottish chronicler, reports on this Daedelus-like attempt:

> . . . he caused make a pair of wings of feathers, which
> being fastened upon him, he flew off the castle wall of
> Stirling, but shortly he fell and broke his thigh bone.

Damian apparently accounted for his failure by the inclusion of:

> . . . some hen feathers in the wings, which yearn
> and covet the midden and not the skies.

This ill-fated attempt attracted the interest of the court poet William Dunbar who observed that Damian indeed found the midden, which rather fortunately broke his fall:

> . . . in a myre, up the ene,
> Amang the glar did glyde.

It must be confessed that although Scotland – in the shape of King James IV – sponsored Damien's attempts the flying Friar was a Frenchman.

Scotland's obsession with science and invention was probably set back, rather than advanced, by the dubious Friar Damien. The first substantial step along the path to the cry of "Beam me up, Scotty" was probably taken by an Edinburgh laird, John Napier of Merchiston. This ingenious Scot invented logarithms and published his work in 1614. By doing so he made complex mathematical calculations relatively simple. In the context of Star Trek's Scotty, it is interesting to note that the earliest significant application of Napier's tables was to astronomy, to such a beneficial effect that the greatest astronomer of the age, Johann Kepler, dedicated a book to Napier. The polymathic Napier also devised a range of "Secrett Inventionis" designed to defeat the Turkish army which was, in the 1590s, threatening Europe. These included a self-propelled tank:

> . . . a round chariot of mettle made of the proof of double muskett, which motion shall be by those that be within the same. . . It serveth to destroy the environed enemy by continuall charge and shott of harquebush through small holes; the enemie in the meantime being abased and altogether uncertaine what defence or pursuit to use against a moving mouth of mettle.

An even more eccentric Scot, Sir Thomas Urquhart, suggests that Napier's infernal device was put to a trial and slaughtered herds of cattle and flocks of sheep, causing its inventor to repent of his work and order its destruction.

Napier must be seen as an isolated figure, albeit a mathematician of world class. With the eighteenth century, however, the Scottish engineer steps into the limelight in quantity as well as in quality. Why Scotland should have become such a centre of the Industrial Revolution is perhaps a question beyond our present argument and our concern here is more with the rise of the engineer to become a potent and universally recognised symbol of Scotland.

If one site can be identified as the first Holy of Holies of the Scottish engineer then that must surely be the Carron Ironworks at Falkirk. Founded in 1759 it soon became both a focus for the industrial revolution and an inescapable stop on the touristic itinerary. Thomas Pennant's enthusiastic reaction was typical:

> Carron iron-works lie about a mile from Falkirk, and are the greatest of the kind in Europe; they were founded about eight years ago, before which there was not a single house, and the country a mere moor. At present, the buildings of all sorts are of vast expense, and above twelve hundred men are employed. The iron is smelted from the stone, then cast into cannon, pots, and all sorts of utensils made in founderies. The work has been of great service to the country, by teaching the people industry and a method of setting about any sort of labour, which before the common people had scarce any notion of.

McAndrew in Kipling's poem prayed:

> Lord, send a man like Robbie Burns to sing the
> Song o' Steam!
> To match wi Scotia's noblest speech yon orchestra sublime.

Burns may never quite have sung the "Song o' Steam" but, like a good traveller, he visited Carron and was prepared to be impressed by the power of the furnaces:

> We cam' na here to view your warks,
> In hope to be mair wise,
> But only, lest we gang to hell,
> It may be nae surprise . . .

In the hundred years after the founding of the Carron works, Scotland was to produce a remarkable succession of great engineers in a variety of disciplines. These men became, in a way it is now difficult to appreciate or to find a modern equivalent for, national hero figures. The story of these men, often from humble backgrounds, became the stuff of myth and improving literature: James Watt (1736-1819), the inventor of the separate condenser for the steam engine and father of the age of steam, but immortalised in legend for watching the kettle boil. Thomas Telford (1757-1834), road and canal builder, aptly nicknamed "The Colossus of Roads". John Rennie (1761-1821) bridge builder and civil engineer – a particularly potent Scottish hero figure as he did most of his work in England; William Symington (1763-1831), pioneer of steam navigation; Henry Bell (1767-1830) originator of Europe's first commercial steam ship.

Bell's life exemplifies the way in which these engineers captured the Scottish imagination. The distressingly untalented weaver-poet, William Harriston, writing a guide to the River Clyde and its newly created steamer services in *The Steam-boat Traveller's Remembrancer* (1824) described Helensburgh:

> There lives Henry Bell, so much fam'd
> For exerting mechanical skill,
> Who the first of our Steam-boats fram'd –
> Thus he merits the nation's good-will.
>
> Far advanc'd in old age is the sire
> Of the Steam-boats in Scotland, yet he
> Retains a great share of the fire
> Of activity, humour and glee. . .

Bell's first biographer, Edward Morris, put his subject's claims on an even higher plane:

> The fire of genius came from heaven
> From Him who David's harp inspir'd –

In love to man, in kindness given,
To raise our world, – Bell's mind was fir'd
With ardent light, mankind to bless;
And patriots will this truth confess.

This is beyond a doubt the portrayal of the engineer as national hero and national role-model – even more, a divinely inspired being. It is surely no coincidence that the greatest Victorian exponent of this type of hero-worshipping biography was a Scot, Samuel Smiles from Haddington in East Lothian, and prominent among his subjects were the Scots Watt, Telford and Rennie.

It is, however, with the rise of the steam-ship and the advent of iron and steel construction that the Scottish self image of the engineer was to find its apotheosis. The emergence of the River Clyde to its late nineteenth-century pre-eminence in world shipbuilding and engineering created both Captains of Industry, and Clyde-trained McAndrews, who represented Scottish enterprise and Scottish skill, in a particularly relevant and identifiable way. The volume of work turned out on the Clyde, the technological innovations developed there, the reputation for quality, all enhanced the reputation of the Scottish engineer and made him into an international stereotype and national personification. It had become accepted that Scotland had a special place in the world of technology. Neil Munro, writing in *The Clyde, River and Firth,* about what he called the "ship shop" of the Clyde observed:

> . . . Clyde steamers, since the marine engine came to
> being, have had a *cachet* like Sheffield cutlery or the
> buns of Bath, so that praise of them is a convention
> of English literature, and Kipling and Conrad, voicing
> the sentiment of the seamen, credit their heroic ships,
> their shrewdest engineers, to the Clyde. . .

Munro goes on to celebrate both the Scots engineer and the Clydeside industrialist:

> Having proved the practicability of propelling ships by steam-driven paddles, local genius sought at once, with Scottish thrift, to do it economically. Men rose then who seemed to give themselves as with poetic ecstasy to the revelation of the power of this new agent in the destiny of man – the Napiers, the Dennys, and the Cairds; John Elder, John Wood, William Pearce; the Thomsons, Todd & McGregor. . .

"As with poetic ecstasy" – perhaps here lies something of the roots of the Scottish obsession with technology. Engineering is being presented by Munro almost as an art form. We are frequently told, with great confidence, that Calvinism or Knox or the Reformation blighted the artistic and cultural life of Scotland. If there is indeed any truth in this somewhat glib assertion, then perhaps Scots found in the ordered working of machines a surrogate art form, and one conformable to the Calvinistic temper of the people:

> From coupler-flange to spindle-guide I see Thy Hand,
>   O God –
> Predestination in the stride o' yon connectin'-rod.

McAndrew even saw in the noise of the engine a divine music:

> . . .the tail-rods mark the time
> The crank-throws give the double-bass, the feed-pump
>   sobs an' heaves,
> An' now the main eccentrics start their quarrel on the
>   sheaves:
> Her time, her own appointed time, the rocking link-head
>   bides,
> Till – hear that note? – the rod's return whings
>   glimmerin' through the guides.

The Scottish convergence between shipbuilding and engineering and fine art was elegantly demonstrated in 1855. That year the Govan yard of Robert Napier launched the strikingly beautiful Cunard liner *Persia* and the designer's sectional plan of *Persia* was exhibited at the Royal Academy in London – the only such technical drawing which had ever been exhibited there.

On a somewhat less rarefied level Macphail, the engineer of Neil Munro's *Vital Spark*, sang the praises of his refitted engine to Para Handy:

> She's a better boat than ever she was. . . Built like a
> lever watch! We'll can get the speed oot o' her noo.
> There's boats gaun up and doon the river wi' red funnels,
> saloon caibins, and German bands in them, that havena
> finer engines. When I get that crank and crossheid
> tightened, thae glands packed and nuts slacked, she'll
> be the gem o' the sea.

Macphail may have been, in his skipper's dismissive phrase:

> . . . only a common fireman. . .

but he would seem to have fully shared in the Scotch obsession with the marine steam engine,

> . . . gie me a good substantial compound engine; nane o'
> your hurdy-gurdies!

he says elsewhere.

While the Scotch ship's engineer (whether steamship or star-ship) is the classic example of the national fascination with technology, he is not the only manifestation of this obsession. The fame of the Stevenson dynasty of lighthouse builders and civil engineers was assured even if young Robert Louis had not deserted the family business, first for the law, and then for literature. But even RLS, rebel and exile in many ways that he was, still responded to the tales of Skerryvore and

Dhu Heartach and loyally celebrated the Stevensons' achievements in *A Family of Engineers*. When, in 1885, Robert Louis Stevenson bought a house in the genteel tranquility of Bournemouth he, somewhat improbably, named it "Skerryvore" after the isolated rock lighthouse built by his ancestors and celebrated both the lighthouse and his new home with a poem:

> For love of lovely words, and for the sake
> Of those, my kinsmen and my countrymen,
> Who early and late in the windy ocean toiled
> To plant a star for seamen, where was then
> The surfy haunt of seals and cormorants:
> I, on the lintel of this cot, inscribe
> The name of a strong tower.

Skerryvore was to RLS a symbol of his family and his nation's engineering achievement. On a national level another major engineering work, another "strong tower", still forms one of the most potent symbols of Scottishness. In the iconography of Scotland, the Forth Bridge stands in the first rank alongside the thistle, tartan, Burns and Bonnie Prince Charlie. The place that this 1890 structure has held in the Scottish imagination could always be judged from its popularity as an image on calendars, postcards, book jackets and shortbread tins. However the storm of controversy which erupted over a ScotRail decision to suspend, as an economy measure, the Bridge's continuous painting programme, revealed it still to be held in great affection and widely cherished as a national emblem. Its significance is far greater than any fiscally calculated assessment of its role in the national railway infrastructure would suggest. The Bridge is seen as a demonstration of Scottish excellence, of confidence, skill and expertise. In an age which has seen the decline of much of the Scottish engineering tradition and the disappearance of much of Scottish heavy industry the Forth Bridge stands for a vanished or vanishing heritage.

In pure and applied science, the Scots have demonstrated a disproportionate degree of success and the national self image has focused on these scientists – emphasising their Scottishness at all costs – even if, like Alexander Graham Bell, another country has high claims on him. After all, most of his work on telephones was done in the United States, where he emigrated to as a young man. The Scottish soul particularly enjoys the "lad o' pairts" story, the scientist from humble background – a James Watt or Sir Alexander Fleming and the inventor who struggles against difficulty – John Logie Baird and television being an excellent example of the latter taste.

Sadly there is all too much evidence at the end of the twentieth century that Scotland's early and much-vaunted predominance in technology has declined almost to vanishing point. Studies show a low level of investment, low rates of introduction of advanced machinery, and even, bitterest of bitter pills, a low level of invention. In 1995 a study conducted by international management consultants Arthur Andersen indicated that Scotland's level of patent registration had sunk to that of Poland or Jordan. The reasons for this decline are seemingly less clear than the simple facts – perhaps the "branch factory" syndrome means that though the creative work is done in Scotland the registration takes place from a "head office" in London or California. What the long term effects of this decline will be on this particular Scotch Obsession is impossible to say. The change from heavy engineering to electronics as the basis for Scotland's productive industry is also an unpredictable element – but it does seem unlikely that the sterile microchip plants of "Silicon Glen" and the new industrial order will attract the same emotional response as the shipyards, foundries and engine-works of the first industrial age. Nor can we safely predict what sort of men will be formed in these new industrial environments. Let Kipling's McAndrew have the last word:

> What I ha' seen since ocean-steam began
> Leaves me na doot for the machine: but what about the man?

THE
STAR-SPANGLED
SCOTCHMAN

The Scots and the
United States of America

T he 1914-18 memorial in Edinburgh's Princes Street
  Gardens. An inscription which reads; "erected as a
tribute from those of Scottish blood and sympathies in
the United States of America to Scotland.

> A people that jeoparded their lives unto the death in
> the high places of the field.
> *Judges V.18*"

A Country and Western club somewhere in West
Central Scotland. A packed crowd of enthusiasts who
have spent the evening listening to Tammy Wynette
and Hank Williams records and watching demonstrations of square dancing and quick-draw expertise. All
stand with heads bowed as the strains of *Dixie* sound
and the flag of the Confederacy, "Old Glory", is lowered
on the flagpole. Afterwards, the members file out in
their crinolines and bootlace ties and buckskins and
check shirts and jeans, and drive off in their cars, some
with the Confederate flag on their bonnets – or should
it be hoods?

Two images, each offering evidence of a deep and
abiding fascination ("sympathies") of each of two
nations with the other's concerns. Obviously this has

something to do with the historic relationship between Scotland and the USA, with the part played by Scots in opening up of the North American continent to Europeans, with the pre-eminence of others among the sons and daughters of the Revolution and with the trans-plantation of the Protestant, i.e. Scottish, work ethic to American soil.

At another level, the relationship has to do with the distinctive contributions of the older country to the science, the culture and the ideas of the newer, of people like Watt, Adam Smith, Robert Adam and others in the age of the Enlightenment, which nurtured the American Revolution, and in a later generation, of John Muir, almost unknown in his native Scotland, but hailed as a new prophet of the environmental principle in the United States.

From the very beginning the relationship was a two-way one, in that young America looked back across the Atlantic as much as Scots fixed their hopes and desires on the New World. A popular song of the 1840s, with its echo of Robert Burns, reflects the latter aspirations:

To the West, to the West, to the land of the free,
Where the mighty Missouri rolls down to the sea;
Where a man is a man even though he must toil
And the poorest may gather the fruits of the soil.

and as sung by Will Carnegie of Dunfermline to his young son Andrew, it expressed the need felt by many Scots to seek an alternative, a fresh start when their hopes for political reform at home were disappointed. For followers of the Chartist Movement, like the Carnegies, the democratic USA seemed a political beacon which attracted them as much as economic reasons drove them until, in the Thirties, 300,000 Scots made the passage to America. Many more looked across the Atlantic for hopes of better days and new horizons , and if example were needed, Andrew Carnegie's story provided it.

This was the classic tale of the poor lad who made a fortune through hard work and other traditional Scottish virtues, and in a way is the old notion of the lad o' pairts played out on a wider stage. Carnegie is remembered more for his philanthropy and capitalism and for the way that he enunciated these new creeds, than for his politics, but in his earliest days the radical tradition comes through loud and clear. Under the influence of his adopted land, however, the radical becomes more of a republican.

> I cannot feel much interest in Kings or in any who occupied or do occupy positions, not by merit, but by birth. Let the successors of such build monuments to their predecessors, or those who can live contentedly under institutions which deny them equality. I am too staunch a Republican, hate with a bitter hatred and resent as an insult to my manhood, the monarchical idea. A king is an insult to every other man in the land.

But Carnegie's brand of republicanism did not find much of an echo in his native land, since radicalism in Scotland owed more to French than American influences and, on the other political wing, at the outset of the Revolution very many Scots in the colonies were fervent in the cause of Empire Loyalism, including, interestingly enough, some, like Flora MacDonald and her husband, who had been active supporters of the Jacobite cause at home.

Carnegie, "the star-spangled Scotchman", illustrates something else, though – the old dictum, that absence make the heart grow fonder.

> What Benares is to the Hindoo, Mecca to the Mohammedan, Jerusalem to the Christian, all that Dunfermline is to me.

For there has always been an excess of sentiment in relations between the two countries, and in particular when they are regarding each other from a distance. The besetting sin of Scottish literature was always supposed to be sentimentality, and the same can now be said of American television. For serious sentimentality one need only look as far as the body of songs which take exile from Scotland as a theme, from the genuine yearning expressed in the *Canadian Boat Song* to tear-jerking ballads like *My Ain Folk*.

> Tho' I'm far beyond the sea,
> Yet my heart will e'er be,
> Back hame in Bonny Scotland,
> Wi' my ain folk.

That kind of nostalgic imagining was and is no doubt commonplace enough, and relatively harmless, but sometimes the role played by one country in the consciousnesss of the other could be seen as more disturbing.

Certainly there have been occasions in the twentieth century when American culture has been seen as a threat to the British or European way of life, although who remembers now the fears in the Fifties that Britain might end up as "the 49th State"? The linguistic magnet that is American English must damage Gaelic and Scots as much as any other language, but Scots have always tended to embrace cultural imperialism when it comes with a bubblegum sticker. In the Thirties and Forties, sophisticated Scots cinema audiences wouldn't be seen dead at a "British picture", far preferring the Hollywood variety (always excepting that apotheosis of kitsch, "Brigadoon"), and Americans have often remarked on the ease with which Scots children can adopt a Transatlantic twang when playing at "Batman" or "Superman". It is on the whole more fashionable to decry this kind of influence as official contacts between the UK and America have waned with the decline of the "Special Relationship".

For their part, it seems that Americans have greater difficulty today in distinguishing Scots from other kinds of "Brits" and it remains to be seen whether *Braveheart* can capture the US imagination with a sense of place as *The Quiet Man* did for the Irish. Similarly, the half-hearted efforts which were made to find Ronald Reagan a tartan were never going to rival the close and very real identification of Jack Kennedy and the Boston Irish with their motherland.

It wasn't always the case, however. In the early years of the Republic, Scottish influence was very strong, even out of proportion to numbers, and a number of Scots were signatories of the Declaration of Independence. Certainly John Witherspoon, a Scots minister and later first president of Princeton University, as well as the first pedant to rage against what he called "Americanisations" of speech, was one of them. Some have speculated about the possible influence upon the American document of a much earlier Declaration, that of Arbroath, in 1320. Compare the proposition:

> . . .that all Men are created equal, that they are endowed by their Creator with certain inalienable rights, that among these are Life, Liberty and the pursuit of Happiness

with:

> We fight not for glory nor for wealth nor honour: but only and alone we fight for Freedom, which no good man surrenders but with his life.

and:

> that to secure these rights, governments are instituted among Men, deriving their just powers from the consent of the governed

which a Scot, Lord Acton, of "absolute power" fame, drew attention to as a truly revolutionary statement, but might also have compared with:

> Yet [King] Robert himself, should he turn aside from
> the task that he has begun, and yield Scotland or us to
> the English King and people, we should cast out as the
> enemy of us all, as subverter of our rights and of his
> own, and should choose another king to defend our
> freedom. . .

In literature, authors as different as Henry Mackenzie, "Ossian" Macpherson and Burns were idolised in the States, and when a personal march tune was sought for the President, it was a setting of *Hail to the Chief* which filled the bill.

> Hail to the Chief who in triumph advances!
> Honoured and blessed be the evergreen Pine!
> Long may the tree, in his banner that glances,
> Flourish, the shelter and grace of our line!

Taken from the Boat Song in *The Lady of the Lake* by Sir Walter Scott, this was symptomatic of the influence of the authors of the Romantic movement upon the US literary, cultural and even political establishment. Not all observers were happy with the latter influence, and it was the impact of Scott in particular upon the consciousness of the South which led to the most famous denunciation of a Scots author by an American writer, or possibly of any author by another anywhere!

Writing in *Life on the Mississippi* (1883), Mark Twain launches the following attack.

> Against the crimes of the French Revolution and of
> Bonaparte may be set two compensating benefactions:
> the Revolution broke the chains of the *ancien regime*
> and of the Church, and made of a nation of abject slaves
> a nation of freemen; and Bonaparte instituted the setting

of merit above birth, and also so completely stripped the
divinity from royalty, that whereas crowned heads in
Europe were gods before, they are only men, since, and
can never be gods again. . .

(An inspiration for Carnegie perhaps?)

Then comes Sir Walter Scott with his enchantments,
and by his single might checks this wave of progress,
and even turns it back; sets the world in love with
dreams and phantoms; with decayed and swinish
forms of religion; with decayed and degraded systems
of government; with the sillinesses and emptinesses,
sham grandeurs, sham gauds, and sham chivalries of
a brainless and worthless long-vanished society.

Great prose from Twain, and certainly the creation of
trivia and fustian tushery was a charge levelled at Sir
Walter even in his lifetime, although, as a good
Presbyterian, he might have jibbed at the the promotion
of "swinish forms of religion"! But what, specifically
has this to do with the mighty USA?

Most of the world has now outlived good part of these
harms, though by no means all of them; but in our
South they flourish pretty forcefully still. . . There, the
genuine and wholesome civilization of the nineteenth
century is curiously confused and commingled with the
Walter Scott Middle-Age sham civilization; and so you
have practical, common-sense, progressive ideas and
progressive works, mixed up withe duel, the inflated
speech, and the jejune romanticism of an absurd past
that is dead, and out of charity ought to be buried.

That's what the makars of the same "Middle-Age" might
have called a flyting. And now a much more serious charge:

But for the Sir Walter disease, the character of the
Southerner – or Southron, according to Sir Walter's

starchier way of phrasing it – would be wholly modern,
in place of modern and medieval mixed, and the South
would be fully a generation further advanced than it is.
For it was he that created rank and caste, and pride and
pleasure in them. Enough is laid on slavery, without
fathering upon it these creations and contributions of
Sir Walter.

And as a consequence of this?

> Sir Walter had so large a hand in making Southern
> character, as it existed before the war, that he is in great
> measure responsible for the [American Civil] war.

And was responsible for the mass slaughter of the first
"modern" war? Just as well he wasn't alive to see what he
had wrought. But now Mark Twain, among the greatest
of humourists, who might have been a Scotophile, as
author of a version of "Finn'" (Huckleberry, not
McCool), proceeds to finish off the Wizard of the North,
and without even a tinge of irony:

> He did measureless harm; more real and lasting harm,
> perhaps, than any other individual that ever wrote.

Whaur's yer Machiavelli, Freud, Hitler and Rushdie
noo? Even, Dorothy Parker, at her most waspish, could
not have aspired to a notice like that.

So, the efforts of the Glenbuck Gunslingers and the
Corstorphine Country and Western Club to keep the
flame of the Old South burning, or at least the flag
flying, is perhaps a kind of belated atonement for the
pernicious effects of one worthy Scots gentleman. Just
as well that it did not occur to Mark Twain to link
Sir Walter and the Scottish inheritance with another
dreadful chapter in American history, although others
have remarked on the links between Scotland and the
Ku Klux Klan. Not simply because of the word "clan"

either, but because, among other things, the "fiery cross" probably came to the "Klansmen" by means of Sir Walter's verses in *The Lady of the Lake* such as

Proudly our pibroch has thrilled in Glen Fruin,
And Bannochar's groans to our slogan replied;
Glen Luss and Ross-dhu, they are smoking in ruin,
And the best of Loch Lomond lie dead on her side.

Of course, that legacy of wrong-doing isn't the warlike Scotch's only contribution to the vocabulary of American infamy. "Blackmail" of course was a contribution of the Border reivers, from their habit of exacting payment of black cattle for not burning the owners out, and if the advertising world can be said to be infamous, too, what about the the perversion of the meaning of "slogan", from full-throated a Highland battle-cry – as in the excerpt above – to the tinny, insistent and empty notes of an advertising jingle?

The Scots contribution was not only to American vocabulary. The War of Independence had a beneficial effect on the village of Larbert in that the fledgling Carron Ironworks were saved from collapse by that war, and the "carronades" didn't all end up on the British side. And fighting on the American side was the boy from Arbigland in Kirkcudbright, the former privateer who founded the US Navy, John Paul Jones. It was said that "the nurses of Scotland hushed their crying charges by the whisper of his name", because of their fears that he would ravage their shores like Blackbeard or Captain Kidd – a Greenock man actually!

As it happened, the Yankees never did come in anger, not even in retaliation for the kilted regiments made to look foolish in the abortive war of 1812, but many of them indeed came in both World Wars, a million GIs in WW2 streaming through the Tail of the Bank, and distributing their favours and gum among the Port

Glasgow weans, having crossed the Atlantic on the great liners built in that same river:

> New York to Gourock 16,683 souls aboard. New York 25 July 1943. Gourock 30 July 1943. 3,353 miles, 4 days, 20 hours, 42 minutes. 28.73 knots. The greatest number of human beings ever embarked on one vessel.
> Extract from Log of RMS *Queen Mary*

Tourists had always visited, of course. Not many from Scotland to the USA, that is until the recent boom in Costa Florida holidays, but mostly from the States, often as part of their Grand Tour of Europe in 20 days. Some American visitors left accounts of their impressions, favourable or not.

> Often these clouds came down and enveloped us in a drizzle, or rather a shower, of such minute drops that they had not weight enough to fall. This, I suppose, was a genuine Scotch mist; and as such it is well enough to have experienced it, though I would willingly never see it again.

That was Nathaniel Hawthorne's view of a Scotch obsession, at least in the telling, in 1870.

To conclude with the words of an American writer, a first generation Scot on both his mother and father's side, best known for his *Moby Dick*, based on his own time on a whaler, when he very likely rubbed shoulders with whaling men from Dundee or Kirkwall – Herman Melville in *Mardi* gives a very partial account of Scotland that must come under the heading of a gentle obsession:

> Our chronicler narrated many fine things of its people; extolling their bravery in war, their amiability in peace, their simplicity and sweetness in song, their loving-kindness and frugality in all things domestic – running over a long catalogue of heroes, metaphysicians, bards, and good men.

A HARDY AND INTREPID RACE

The Scots and War

General James Wolfe, between assisting the Duke of Cumberland to win the Battle of Culloden in 1746 and dying picturesquely on the Heights of Abraham in Canada in 1759, had occasion to write of the Highland soldiers who were then being recruited into the British Army:

> They are a hardy and intrepid race. . .

but unfortunately went on to add the cynical rider:

> . . . and no great mischief if they fall.

His political master, Lord Barrington, the Secretary at War, wrote in a similar vein:

> I am for having always in our army as many Scottish soldiers as possible; not that I think them more brave. . . but because they are generally more hardy and less mutinous: and of all Scottish soldiers I should choose to have and keep. . . as many Highlanders as possible.

These two English observers of the abilities of the Scots as fighting men might have been speaking of a highly superior sort of domestic animal – bred for strength and loyalty – but there is little doubt that their views of the talents of the Scots for war were and are shared by the

Scots themselves. In fact the self image of the Scot, from Barbour's "Bruce" to Andy Stewart's "A Scottish Soldier" and the Edinburgh Military Tattoo, closely accords with the perception of Barrington and Wolfe. One of the earliest recorded examples of the Scotch obsession with their own military genius and predilection for warfare comes in 1385 and is found in the chronicles of the Flemish priest, historian, traveller and diplomat, Jean de Froissart. Froissart tells of a French army sent to Scotland under the terms of the Auld Alliance, to assist Robert II in his war with England. The Scots, Froissart suggests, were less than grateful for the arrival of their French allies. Indeed some Scots were soon heard to say:

> What devil has brought them here, or who has sent for them? Cannot we carry on our wars with England without their assistance?. . . Let them be told to return again, for we are sufficiently numerous in Scotland to fight our own quarrels, and do not want their company.

It is interesting that elsewhere in his *Chronicles* Froissart reports that:

> The Scots are bold, hardy, and much inured to war

and explains how, on their cross-border raids into England they subsist mainly on oatmeal bannocks, a little meat and water, concluding that:

> . . . it is therefore no wonder, that they perform a longer day's march than other soldiers

- a pragmatic recommendation that would surely have appealed to Wolfe and Barrington.

It is probably an essential component of the Scottish self image as a warlike race that we are, of course, only warlike when forced to be – a splendid example of this conceit comes in that most stirring piece of propaganda, *The Declaration of Arbroath*. First of all, Scotland is presented as the pure and innocent nation:

> . . . Edward, King of England, . . . finding our realm
> without a king, and our people innocent of evil intent
> and still unused to the assaults of war, came to us in
> the guise of a friend and ally and then made a hostile
> attack on us. . .

The document then argues that if we are forced to fight,
then by heavens we will do so with might and main:

> . . . we have been delivered by our most valiant Prince
> and King, Robert; who, that he might free his people
> and heritage from the hands of the enemy, rose like
> another Joshua or Maccabeus, and cheerfully endured
> toil and weariness, hunger and peril. . .

A "hardy and intrepid race" indeed! But beware, the
Declaration says, the Scots when roused are dangerous,
even though we are an innocent and harmless people who:

> . . . live on the uttermost bounds of human habitation
> and covet nothing but our own. . .

because:

> For so long as one hundred men remain alive, we
> shall never under any circumstances submit to the
> domination of the English. It is not for glory or riches
> or honours that we fight, but only for liberty, which
> no good man will consent to lose but with his life.

An important element in the Scottish self-image as a
warrior race must come from the deeds of Wallace and
Bruce and the early literature surrounding these deeds,
particularly the writings of Blind Harry and John Barbour:

> . . . we haf the richt;
> And for the richt ilk man suld ficht. . .
> . . . we for our lyvis
> And for our childer and our wifis,

And for the fredome of our land
Ar strenyeit in battale for to stand. . .

These lines from Barbour's *The Bruce* put the Wars of Independence into the context of a principled campaign for national liberation and the depiction of the heroic deeds of Wallace, Bruce and "gud Schyr James off Douglas" have been enormously influential in the development of a national consciousness and military obsessiveness.

However the Scottish tendency to warlike behaviour has not been confined to our own land – or to that of our immediate neighbours. Scottish military expertise and manpower has, throughout the centuries, been an export trade. At times this has been a matter of public policy – as during the Hundred Years War when Scottish armies were sent to France to assist in the French war of national liberation – at other times it was more of, literally, a free-lance exercise. Perhaps the formation by the French Kings of their *Garde Ècossaise* represents the best-known example of this trade, but for centuries Scots regiments were to be found fighting in most of Europe's wars. Indeed the origins of the oldest regiment in the British Army – the Royal Scots – lies in just such an arrangement. In 1633 John Hepburn of Athelstaneford was given permission to raise a regiment for service with Louis XIII of France. After some 45 years' service the *Regiment d'Hebron* ceased to be part of the French army and came home to become, eventually the Royal Scots, the 1st Regiment of Foot. Hepburn's men might well have fought fellow-countrymen in the service of rival monarchs – indeed with Scots regiments in the service of Bohemia, Sweden, Holland, etc. it would be well nigh impossible not to.

Douglas Young recounts Professor R.W. Seton-Watson's story of a border dispute in Bessarabia between the Russian and Ottoman Empires, a tale which points up the possibilities produced by the Scottish military Diaspora. A Russian General and a Turkish Pasha met to discuss the border dispute and carried out their negotiations in the international language of diplomacy – French. A satisfactory outcome having been reached the Russian General turned to the Turkish Pasha and enquired:

"Weel, Jock, and foo's aa wi ye in Inverurie"

a tale which admirably reflects the number of soldiers and sailors who left Scotland, willingly or as exiles and entered foreign service.

This trade in soldiers continued into the eighteenth century, being given something of a fillip by the Jacobite movement – Alan Breck Stewart in Stevenson's *Kidnapped* explains how the system worked. He had to travel between Scotland and France, carrying his chief's rents and messages between the Jacobite court in exile and the Highlands, but:

Whiles I pick up a few lads to serve the King of France: recruits, ye see; and that's aye a little money.

Quite why Scotland should have been such a fertile source for soldiers, or why the profession of arms so appealed to Scots is a point worth exploring. Samuel Johnson had, as usual, no doubts about the matter:

Mountaineers are warlike, because by their feuds and competitions they consider themselves as surrounded with enemies, and are always prepared to repel incursions, or to make them. Among a warlike people, the quality of highest esteem is personal courage, and with the ostentatious display of courage are closely connected promptitude of offence and quickness of resentment.

Not that Johnson was the only observer to make such a comment; in the Middle Ages the *praefervidum ingenium*

Scotorum – the fervent nature of the Scots, was well-observed and our French allies described a touchy person as being *fier comme un Écossais* – as proud as a Scotsman. However there seems no doubt that, racial stereotypes aside, the main motivation for recruitment was economic necessity and the inability of rural areas to sustain an excess of population.

The Highlands, as perhaps the main breeding ground for soldierly export, had a long military tradition. Clan chiefs measured their standing, not by acres or bank balances, but by the number of armed men they could muster:

> That dignity which they derived from an opinion of
> their military importance, the law, which disarmed
> them, has abated.

observed Dr Johnson. As a consequence the Scot, and particularly the Highland Scot, was bred up to the use of arms. Even in the Lowlands the regularity with which cross-Border belligerence took place, whether full-scale invasion or Border reiving, produced a race as handy with the sword and the bill as with plough and the spade. The Border reivers considered that cattle theft and raiding was an everyday part of life, a view also held by such noted extractors of blackmail and black cattle as Rob Roy MacGregor.

The profession of arms was thus, in Scotland, an honourable calling. England may have had to fill up its regiments with the sweepings of the gaols and what Wellington would call "the scum of the earth" but Scottish regiments were of a different character. How different may be judged from the Cameronians with their regimental Kirk Session, an elder drawn from every company and every man carrying a Bible. Equally revealing of a different social order was the command issued to the Highland Brigade by Sir Colin Campbell before the Battle of Alma in the Crimean War:

> No soldier must go carrying off wounded men. If any
> soldier does such a thing his name shall be stuck up
> in his parish church.

The force of such a threat depended on the soldier being a respect-worthy person, an integrated part of society, not a drop-out or reject from society.

The military life was thus in an earlier age both an economic necessity and a respectable career, neither of which would account for its continuing role as a Scotch Obsession. This, paradoxically, probably owes more to the post-Union, indeed post-Culloden, period than it does to the romantic vision of the Scots Archers in medieval France or even the exploits of Wallace and Bruce. From the late eighteenth century some of the most powerful images of Scotland and Scottishness have been associated with the Scottish soldier. One need only think of the charge of the Royal Scots Greys at Waterloo and Sergeant Ewart's capture of the French colours for a potent image – and one memorably captured in Lady Butler's epic painting. Equally memorable and equally symbolic are the Thin Red Line of the Sutherland Highlanders at Balaclava, the sound of the pipes at the Relief of Lucknow, the picture of Piper Findlater, shot through both ankles, playing the Gordons into action at Dargai on the North West Frontier of India and winning the Victoria Cross. These, and a score of other episodes, became immortalised in song, story and shortbread tin. Why?

With the growing incorporation of Scotland into a United Kingdom, with the blurring of the age-old line of demarcation between England and Scotland, with the emergence of a world-wide British Empire, the distinctiveness of the Scottish soldier – the tartan, the kilt, the trews, the pipes; provided a valuable and convenient emblem of Scottish individuality and identity. It was, besides, a safe emblem, a Scottishness that was unthreatening to the established order, a Scottishness that was securely contained within the British polity, an individuality that was endorsed, and thus sanitised, by the highest ranks in the British social order. Thus the 91st Highlanders (later the 1st Argyll & Sutherland Highlanders) were honoured by Queen Victoria by allowing them to add her daughter, Princess Louise's, name to the regimental title.

If the Empire embraced and absorbed the Scottish soldier and the Scottish people saw their soldiers as an acceptable expression of Scottishness, there is no doubt that, equally, the Scots seized all the opportunities that the Empire offered and took on the role of Imperial policeman with enthusiasm. The American historian, Wallace Notestein gives a fascinating account in *The Scot in History*, of a striking example of the mutual fascination of the Scot and the military life:

> It is said that from 1797 to 1837, the Island of Skye
> alone, a small fraction of the Highlands, gave to the
> British army twenty-one lieutenant- and major-generals,
> forty-eight lieutenant-colonels and six hundred other
> commissioned officers, and ten thousand men in the
> ranks.

Of course in the rational twentieth century the Scotch Obsession with things military has vanished. Well, perhaps not! In 1968 one of the many series of post-war military force reductions proposed the disbandment of the Argyll & Sutherland Highlanders – a proposal which occasioned a massive and eventually successful public campaign to "Save the Argylls". In the 1990s the "Peace Dividend", the planned savings resulting from the ending of the Cold War, saw another round of planned cuts in the armed forces. The proposal to merge the Gordon Highlanders with the Queen's Own Highlanders (Seaforth & Camerons) provoked yet another national campaign with meetings, endless letters to the newspapers, petitions, car stickers, and all the apparatus of modern protest. A parallel proposal to merge the Kings Own Scottish Borderers with the Royal Scots drew a similar reaction – a reaction which was by no means confined to old soldiers, Colonel Blimps and the political right. The result was a draw – the KOSBs retained their independent status but the Gordons were merged.

One final thought on this obsession – it is surely something of a triumph for the national spirit that the Scots can have sustained an obsessive interest in war and the military on such a poor track record. What have, to name but ten random examples, the Battles of Brunanburgh, the Standard, Dunbar, Falkirk, Methven, Neville's Cross, Flodden, Solway Moss, Pinkie, and Dunbar (again!) got in common. The answer is, of course, that they are just some of the significant Scottish defeats at the hands of the "auld enemy". Even the most partisan of historians would find it hard to argue that the Scots were not more often defeated than they were victorious, so why does our military obsession have such force? The answer to this may lie in that all purpose, if unspellable, concept of Scottish Antisyzygy – an obsession which we deal with elsewhere.

THE STRANGE CASE OF DR JEKYLL AND MR HYDE

Caledonian Antisyzygy

As a race Scots, it seems, have a constant need to explain their national character to others, but also to themselves. In doing this they might be supposed to wish to present themselves in as good a light as possible, but that, while largely true, has some qualifications. They may suggest, for example, that there are limits to their beneficence – while stressing their generosity and hospitality they will, as we have seen, at the same time be happy to retell stories about the caution or meanness of fellow Scots. Similarly, the quality of life in Scotland might be praised one minute and in the next described as an extreme of poverty. Indeed, in all of this they would tend to take up extreme positions, to give a hint of the national tendency towards obsession, toward "gaun yer dinger", "giein' it laldy", thrawnness, snatching defeat from the jaws of victory (*cf.* Battle of Dunbar, international football, etc.), paranoia and the like.

So, is this ability to reveal more than one aspect of the national psyche indication of a rare magnanimity of vision perhaps? Is the Scots character a nice counterpoint of different emphases and enthusiasms, or does such a view fail to take account of the real dynamic of the obsessions to which such a character is prone? The dynamic suggested to some observers is not one of equilibrium, of harmonious relationships, but rather of a more violent kind of tension. Hugh MacDiarmid's adoption of the term Caledonian antisyzygy might seem appropriate here. This idea captures the extreme form of tension represented in the Scots character and suggests the dichotomy between conflicting opposites which is so much a feature of the country's life and culture, and indeed is found in MacDiarmid's work and constitutes a recurrent theme, conscious or not, in the work of many other Scottish writers. G. Gregory Smith, who coined the phrase, writing in *Scottish Literature* in 1919 expressed this view:

> We need not be surprised to find that in his literature
> the Scot presents two aspects which appear contradic-
> tory. Oxymoron was ever the bravest figure, and we
> must not forget that disorderly order is order after all.

To take two well-known examples: Robert Louis Stevenson mined this rich seam within the Scottish consciousness when he produced the prototype of a whole line of tales of horror in *The Strange Case of Dr Jekyll and Mr Hyde* and built his plot round the idea of contrasting and antipathetic elements. Earlier, James Hogg had shown that an extreme and perverted Calvinist cast of mind could provide a fascinating source of inspiration to a novelist and in *The Confessions of a Justified Sinner* produced what is arguably one of the earliest and greatest psychological studies in world literature.

Antisyzygy is at least a term which we can use to characterise certain forms of creativity. To what extent, however, is it representative of the Scottish character in general and is it equally appropriate at all times in Scotland's history? If it is to be given wider application it will be necessary to examine some possible causes of this tension or dichotomy. Hogg's novel suggests one influence which undoubtedly has a bearing on this

notion of antisyzygy – that is the part played by the
Calvinist conscience. There have been very many
individuals affected by it, such as the poet Robert
Fergusson, author of "Auld Reekie" and "The Daft
Days". From producing uninhibitedly joyous lines such
as these from the latter work. . .

> Whan merry Yule-day comes, I trow,
> You'll scantlins find a hungry mou;
> Sma' are our cares, our stamacks fou
> O gusty gear,
> And kickshaws, strangers to our view
> Sin' fairn-year.

> Ye browster wives! now busk ye braw,
> And fling your sorrows far awa;
> Then, come and gie's the tither blaw
> O' reaming ale,
> Mair precious than the Well o' Spa,
> Our hearts to heal.

. . .at the height of his popularity, he suddenly deserted
his muse, fell into a religious mania and amongst his
ravings denounced "the miscreants who had crucified
our Saviour". Fergusson, who died at the age of
twenty-three in 1774, could be said to have suffered the
effects of a Calvinist or Presbyterian guilt complex, as
a modern psychoanalyst might put it. Indeed, the
religious consciousness, Calvinist or not, is a recurrent
motif in the Scottish psyche and religious obsession,
too, has been one focus of attention in this book.

It is possible, of course, that the religious conscience
is itself a manifestation rather than a cause or reason of
antisyzygy. So, since we cannot be certain whether it
is cause or effect, other factors have been examined.
One such is the relationship with the geography and
topography of Scotland, together with various other
associated historical and political factors. The fact that

Scotland marches with England, that it shares a border with a larger southern neighbour, has been a determinant of national temperament throughout history.

Looking at a time before the establishment of the kingdom of Scotland, feelings of being exposed at the extremity of these islands, at the end of the world even, threatened by powerful enemies, might be detected, if a little fancifully, in this account given by the Roman historian Tacitus of a speech by Calgacus (The Swordsman), one of the Caledonian leaders at the time of Mons Graupius around the year 84:

> There is now no nation beyond us, nothing save the
> billows and the rocks and the Romans, still more savage
> . . . when they make a wilderness they call it peace.

And so on down the centuries the people of Scotland were to develop unwillingly the dichotomy of mind and spirit which was the product of alternating periods of peace and war and the relentless tensions of border-lands. The unknown thirteenth-century poet lamenting the death of Alexander III might be expressing apprehension about these tensions:

> Crist, born in virgynyte,
> Succour Scotlande, and ramede,
> That is stade in perplexite.

Bannockburn and the Declaration of Arbroath only gave promise of a false dawn and more often than not there were the recurrent trauma resulting from the dashing of hopes by one crushing invasion or another. Jane Elliot's "The Flowers of the Forest" is, of course, not contemporary with Flodden, most emphatic of all defeats, but does suggest the overwhelming melancholic aspect of Caledonian antisyzygy:

> In hairst, at the shearing, nae youths now are jeering
> Bandsters are runkled and lyart or grey:

At fair or at preaching, nae wooing, nae fleeching
The flowers of the Forest are a' wede away

We'll hear nae mair lilting at the yowe-milking;
Women and bairns are heartless and wae,
Sighing and moaning on ilka green loaning
The Flowers of the Forest are a' wede away.

As to the contrasting, more euphoric or even humorous side, there is precious little evidence of that in much of Scotland's political relationships, unless we include the bitter irony which infused the popular term for one particularly dreadful passage of arms during the minority of Mary, Queen of Scots. As a kind of savage jest, this was dubbed "The Rough Wooing" and at a time when the English Privy Council could issue the almost laconic instruction:

Put all to fyre and swoorde. . . burn Edinborough
towne, so rased and defaced when ye have sacked
and gotten what ye can of it, as there may remayne
forever a perpetuel memory of the vengeance of God.

No doubt there would be occasions of roistering and even happiness, but the note of irony and satire runs through nearly all Scottish attempts at humour. A good example is the simultaneous awarding of the epithets "Bloody Clavers" and "Bonnie Dundee" to John Graham of Claverhouse, Viscount Dundee, who could almost be seen as a paradigm of the particular obsession we are examining. Incidentally, the old ballad which celebrates Dundee's last battle at Killiecrankie contains an image which is somehow symbolic of the idea of antisyzygy, and certainly brings to mind a scene from Hogg's *The Confessions of a Justified Sinner*, with the figure of Wringhim side by side with his doppelganger Gil-Martin:

I fought at land, I fought at sea,
At hame I fought my auntie-o;
But I met the devil and Dundee
On the braes o' Killiecrankie-o.

As has been said, irony and satire seems to predominate in the consciousness and literature of this beleaguered race. Look, for example, at Sir David Lyndsay's magnificent verse satire, "The Thrie Estates" – although Lyndsay has his more humorous moments. Not until the calmer waters of the mid-eighteenth-century are reached can a poet like Burns relax a little in the merrier warmth of a "Tam o' Shanter", even though he still can employ the biting wit in satirical verses such as "Holy Willie", directed against the old enemy of excessive Calvinism:

I bless and praise thy matchless might,
When thousands Thou has left in night,
That I am here before Thy sight,
For gifts and grace
A burning and a shining light,
To a' this place.

What was I, or my generation,
That I should get such exaltation?
I, wha deserved most just damnation
For broken laws,
Sax thousand years ere my creation
Thro' Adam's cause.

If the fact of the existence of the Border with England contributed to the dichotomy or antisyzygy we have been examining, so to did the existence of another, and in some senses wider and deeper cultural and racial gulf – the one between Lowland and Highland Scotland.

Here we touch upon some of the longest-standing ambiguities in the national identity, where, for example, even the word "Scot" itself can have had different layers of meaning imposed upon it at different periods, and nationality is or has been quite an elusive thing. Back in the early fifteenth century the divisions between Celtic and Lowland Scotland were very marked indeed. The Battle of Harlaw in 1411 was one episode in the fierce rivalry between the Islemen of the West under Donald Lord of the Isles and one of the chief magnates of (mainland) Scotland, the Earl of Mar. In John Major's *History of Greater Britain* (another ambiguity in that title!) the term Scots is reserved for Mar's followers, although paradoxically the original Scots of the Dark Ages had hailed from Ireland and first settled in the Hebrides:

> The civilised Scots. . . did not put Donald to open rout,
> though they fiercely strove, and not without success,
> to put a check to the audaciousness of the man.

As the reader will have read, the Stewart kings believed they had a mission to put down rebellions in the Celtic regions, in a typically feudal fashion, by enforcing an unrealistic homogeneity, although James IV, for one, was known to "have the Gaelic" as well as Scots. Not until much later at the close of the period of Jacobite rebellions was political power in a position to begin the dismantling of Gaelic cultural identity. Dr Samuel Johnson described firstly some of the distinctive features of character in people living in remote wild country. . .

> Mountainous regions are sometimes so remote from the
> seat of government, and so difficult of access, that they
> are very little under the influence of the sovereign, or
> within the reach of national justice. Law is nothing
> without power; and the sentence of a distant court
> could not be easily executed, nor perhaps very safely
> promulgated, among men ignorantly proud and habitu-
> ally violent, unconnected with the general system, and
> accustomed to reverence only their own lords.

. . . and then was able to make more acute observations about the far-reaching effects produced by the collapse of Highland military power after Culloden in 1746:

> There was perhaps never any change of national manners so quick, so great, and so general, as that which has operated in the Highlands, by the last conquest, and the subsequent laws. . .The clans retain little now of their original character, their ferocity of temper is softened, their military ardour is extinguished, their dignity of independence is depressed, their contempt of government subdued, and the reverence for their chiefs abated. Of what they had before the late conquest of their country, there remain only their language and their poverty.

Johnson's passage suggests another factor which has operated upon the "Caledonian" consciousness, namely poverty. It is true that much of Scotland's history has been characterised by "feast or famine", but with precious little in the way of feast, we might decide that we have had enough bad news for the moment. In any case, obtaining clear information about the real life of the people is never easy. Sometimes we have to use indirect approaches, such as an examination of Scotland's vast fund of ballad and song.

Once again, however, we have to report that the ballads do not offer a very cheery prospect either. Most of them seem to provide further evidence that life was nasty, brutish and short, as in the cases of *Lord Randal* and *Bessie Bell* and *Mary Gray* and the agonising hopelessness of Edward, with just the occasional touch of grim humour again:

> "And what will ye leave to your bairns and your wife,
> Edward, Edward?
> And what will ye leave to your bairns and your wife,

When ye gang owre the sea, O?" –
"The warld's room: let them beg through life,
Mither, mither;
The warld's room: let them beg through life;
For them never mair will I see, O."

As to the settings of the ballads, both of the previously mentioned borderlands feature in the ballad collections and it seems that the tensions operating at a political level there were communicated through this stark and striking oral heritage. For example:

This deed was done at the Otterbourne
About the breaking of the day;
Earl Douglas was buried at the braken bush,
And the Percy led captive away

comes from one of the Anglo-Scottish Border ballads, *The Battle of Otterbourne*.

Interestingly, a third kind of borderland which has a psychological import and is relevant to this discussion, makes an appearance among some of the ballads. *Thomas the Rhymer* and *Tam Lin*, for example, tell of mortals passing over into or meeting inhabitants of Fairyland.

There came a wind out o' the north,
A sharp wind and a snell,
A dead sleep it came over me
And frae my horse I fell;
And the Queen o' Fairies she took me
In yon green hill to dwell.

It has been argued persuasively that this other parallel universe may be connected with pre-Christian, pagan beliefs and could have offered folk a release or escape from the dictates of an authoritarian church. Here, too, the modern mind might detect another contributing factor towards antisyzygy in the Scottish psyche.

In the seventeenth century the Reverend Robert Kirk of Aberfoyle wrote about Fairyland in *The Secret Commonwealth*. However, as a minister of religion, he was open to charges that, rather than maintaining a balance, he was guilty of hypocrisy. This might lead us to the question – how does antisyzygy show itself in individuals, and is the holding of mutually exclusive points of view, of apparently irreconcilable opposites, simply a more polite way of saying that the Scots are hypocrites? Considering the cases of four individuals from different points in our history might help to resolve this.

Firstly, to consider James VI and I – "two kings in one" and "the wisest fool in Christendom" – both his title and the best-known epithet attached to him suggest ambiguity. James stands between two eras and as a Janus-like gatekeeper to two kingdoms; a king who reigned long in Scotland and long again in a newer much-expanded kingdom; a gatekeeper, too, to that other world of the ballads, as author of a treatise on *Demonologie* and as persecutor of witches; a king who spoke Scots but set in train the decline of that language with the English Authorized Version of the Bible. As a man caught between two contrasting visions of king- ship, James had been styled "King of Scots" in the democratic northern fashion but, when transplanted south, moved towards the totalitarian doctrine of "The Divine Right of Kings". He also held no especial brief for the land of his birth.

> Here I sit and govern with my pen. I write and it is done, and by a clearke of the Councill I govern Scotland now, which others could not doe by the sword.
> *Speech to English Parliament, 1607*

The story of James Boswell, greatest of biographers, has an added zest which comes from the revelations long after his death that he enjoyed a fascinating "secret life" which came to light with the discovery in this century of a vast corpus of confidential journals and other papers. As a statement of the guilt-ridden, morbidly-introspective aspect of antisyzygy nothing could better Boswell:

> What he (Garrick the actor) meant by my being a great man I can understand. For really, to speak seriously, I think there is a blossom about me of something more distinguished than the generality of mankind. But I am much afraid that this blossom will never swell into fruit, but will be nipped and destroyed by many a blighting heat and chilling frost. Indeed, I sometimes indulge noble reveries of having a regiment, of getting into Parliament, making a figure, and becoming a man of consequence in the state. But these are checked by dispiriting reflections on my melancholy temper and imbecility of mind. Yet I may probably become sounder and stronger as I grow up. Heaven knows. I am resigned. I trust to Providence.

A more gentle mixture of "humours" was to be found in the Reverend George MacLeod, one of the greatest Scots of the twentieth century. Minister at Govan in the Thirties, he was a pacifist and most eloquent of all nuclear disarmers who had won the Military Cross in battle, who was a convinced socialist and inherited a baronetcy whose title he never used but eventually accepted a life peerage. A constant critic of the Church of Scotland, he yet became Moderator in 1957; the foundation of the Iona Community and his resolution to restore the ruins of St Columba's Abbey on Iona, using the skills of the unemployed and in fulfilment of Columba's prophecy that "Iona shall be as it was", provided the perfect counterpoint to the stark social problems and human waste he had witnessed in his ministry in the Glasgow of the Depresssion. As he vowed,

> It would be the modern counterpart of St Columba's
> original intention: the New Light of Protestantism
> would be lit to meet our day, as his Lamp met his.

This leaves us with the thought that antisyzygy need not be seen as a traumatic condition, that there are really some quite likeable forms of hypocrisy or, if you prefer, that it is possible to hold opposing elements in life and character together and fuse them, as it were, in creative enterprise or work. Robert Burns, who had many seemingly irreconcilable and obsessive sides to his character, who was at the same time a callous fornicator and author of the tenderest of love-lyrics, had this capacity to fuse together wildly contrasting impulses. He was able to make poetry which took the most ordinary everyday incidents and the lowest dregs of society and translated them into jewelled moments and almost god-like beings – a kind of apotheosis, like in the cantata, *The Jolly Beggars*:

> When lyart leaves bestrow the yird,
> Or wavering like the bauckie-bird,
> Bedim cauld Boreas' blast;
> When hailstanes drive with bitter skyte,
> And infant frosts begin to bite,
> In hoary cranreuch drest;
> Ae nicht at e'en a merry core
> O' randie, gangrel bodies,
> In Poosie Nansie's held the splore,
> To drink their orra duddies:
> Wi' quaffing and laughing,
> They ranted an' they sang,
> Wi' jumping an' thumping,
> The vera girdle rang.

Conclusion

. . . that garret of the earth – that knuckle-end of
England – that land of Calvin, oatcakes and sulphur.

In such dismissive terms did Sydney Smith, English
clergyman, wit and writer dismiss Scotland. His
contemporary, the essayist William Hazlitt wrote:

> Among ourselves, the Scotch, as a nation, are
> particularly disagreeable. They hate every appearance
> of comfort themselves and refuse it to others. Their
> climate, their religion, and their habits are equally
> averse to pleasure. Their manners are either distin-
> guished by a fawning sycophance (to gain their own
> ends, and conceal their natural defects), that makes
> one sick; or by a morose, unbending callousness,
> that makes one shudder.

All of which simply goes to prove that obsessions cut
two ways – if the Scots have their obsessions, about
drink and religion, land and literature, and, of course,
the English, then others have their obsessions about the
Scots, and in so doing confirm the validity of discussing
and analysing national obsessions.

In compiling *Scotch Obsessions* we lie open to the
charge that a nation of five million cannot all be
expected to share in one common set of beliefs, that
people are more various and multifaceted than such a
reductionist attitude would suggest; and, of course,
there is a certain truth in this. It might be hard to find a
Scot who fully shared in all of what we have identified
as Scotch obsessions – some indeed, like the present
authors, are free from them all, being quite remarkably

sane, well-balanced and non-obsessive. However, even the least obsessive of Scots cannot fail to have been influenced by some of the obsessions they see around them and our analysis of these obsessions can be read as either a dreadful warning or as a text-book of required behaviour – a sort of manual of Scottishness.

It is no part of our case that the obsessions detailed in this book are the only Scotch obsessions – it would be possible to write at some length on the Scotch obsession with work, perhaps as a particular species of the Protestant Work Ethic. It would be equally possible to examine the Scotch obsession with Ireland and the Irish. The sea also offers great possibilities for Scottish obsessiveness – any nation which can produce the myth of the selkie, the seal people, clearly has something going for it in the deep waters. Obviously some obsessions, though shared in fully by the Scots, are universal ones – and here one thinks, perhaps inevitably, of sex, even if the twentieth-century Scots poet, Alexander Scott defined Scotch Sex as:

> In atween
> Drinks

and it must be remembered that the old Scots proverb has it that:

> Bitin' and scartin' are Scotch folk's wooin'

so perhaps the Scotch obsession with sex has its own national characteristics after all.

What we would certainly claim is that the obsessions we have discussed collectively and individually have had a significant impact on the Scottish character and have influenced both the way that we see ourselves and the way that others – Sydney Smith and William Hazlitt, for example – have chosen to see us. The one thing that these obsessions might be thought to have in common is a tendency towards the retrospective vision – to looking back, to nostalgia, to the year that's awa', to thoughts of the auld wife ayont the fire at Stuckavrallachan, to the days of auld lang syne. There seems little doubt that a major component in what Robert Louis Stevenson called:

> . . . a strong Scotch accent of the mind

is just this relationship with the past, a relationship which, in *The Weir of Hermiston*, he expressed in words we have already quoted, but which bear repetition in this context:

> For that is the mark of the Scot of all classes: that he stands in an attitude towards the past unthinkable to Englishmen, and remembers and cherishes the memory of his forebears, good or bad; and there burns alive in him a sense of identity with the dead even to the twentieth generation.

It is interesting to find this view of the Scots and their relationship to the past and to their ancestry being confirmed in the writings of one of the most English of Englishmen, G.K. Chesterton, even if Chesterton manages to put a somewhat sour face on the phenomenon:

> For Scotland has a double dose of the poison called heredity; the sense of blood in the aristocrat, and the sense of doom in the Calvinist.

It is surely no accident that the historical novel, as a genre, was virtually invented by Walter Scott, or that much of the poetry which put Scotland on the international literary map was essentially historical. The Waverley Novels broke new ground in depicting the people and events of an earlier period, indeed the very sub-title of *Waverley*, "'tis sixty years since", clearly emphasised the author's subject and approach. Similarly in the Ossianic poetry of Macpherson the subject matter is found in a remote historical or legendary period. Walter Scott's early reputation was gained as a poet and his great epic poems such as *Marmion* and *The Lady of the Lake* recounted the tales of border warfare and highland raid for a mass audience in a way that is difficult to imagine contemporary poetry achieving:

> Proudly our pibroch has thrill'd in Glen Fruin,
> And Bannochar's groans to our slogan replied;
> Glen Luss and Ross-dhu, they are smoking in ruin,
> And the best of Loch-Lomond lie dead on her side.
> Widow and Saxon maid
> Long shall lament our raid,
> Think of Clan-Alpine with fear and with woe;
> Lennox and Leven-glen
> Shake when they hear again
> "Roderick Vich Alpine dhu, ho! ieroe!"

The fashion in poetry has moved from the epic and the narrative to the lyric and to introspection, but when Scott dominated early nineteenth century poetry it was with epic historical narrative and the ballad.

Burns might be thought of as a more "modern" lyric poet but his role as a collector, transcriber and editor of older Scottish songs is completely consistent with this over-arching Scotch Obsession with the past and the desire to see the incorporation of literature into a sense of national identity:

> Ev'n then a wish (I mind its power)
> A wish, that to my latest hour
> Shall strongly heave my breast;
> That I for poor auld Scotland's sake
> Some useful plan, or book could make,
> Or sing a sang at least.

Without over-estimating the present book we hope that we, too, "for poor auld Scotland's sake", have succeeded in incorporating literature into a sense of national identity and in using literature to cast some light on those dark corners of the national soul, those itchy scabs we so like to pick at – those wonderful, vexing, deplorable, indispensable Scotch Obsessions.